Getting to Know God

Getting to Know God

An Introduction to Christian Theology

ELISHEVA MECHANIC

RESOURCE *Publications* · Eugene, Oregon

GETTING TO KNOW GOD
An Introduction to Christian Theology

Copyright © 2021 Elisheva Mechanic. All rights reserved. Except for brief quotations in critical publications or reviews, no part of this book may be reproduced in any manner without prior written permission from the publisher. Write: Permissions, Wipf and Stock Publishers, 199 W. 8th Ave., Suite 3, Eugene, OR 97401.

Resource Publications
An Imprint of Wipf and Stock Publishers
199 W. 8th Ave., Suite 3
Eugene, OR 97401

www.wipfandstock.com

PAPERBACK ISBN: 978-1-6667-0946-9
HARDCOVER ISBN: 978-1-6667-0947-6
EBOOK ISBN: 978-1-6667-0948-3

JUNE 22, 2021

Copyright Requirements for Use of Scriptures:

No Permission Required:
KJV- King James Version, Open domain, no copyright required.

THB – The Holy Bible, Translated from Ancient Eastern Manuscripts, copyright © 1957 By A J Holman Company. Copyright has expired — no permission required.

Conditions of Use:
ESV- English Standard Version. Scripture quotations are from The Holy Bible, English Standard Version (ESV), Copyright ©2001 by Crossway Bibles, a publishing ministry of Good News Publishers. Used by permission. All rights reserved.

NIV- New International Version. Scripture taken from the HOLY BIBLE, NEW INTERNATIONAL VERSION, Copyright, © 1973, 1978, 1984 by The International Bible Society. Used by permission, Zondervan Publishing House. All rights reserved.

NRSV – New Revised Standard Version: The Scripture quotations contained herein are from the New Revised Standard Version Bible. Copyright © 1989, by the Division of Christian Education of the National Churches of Christ in the USA. Used by permission. All rights reserved

This book is dedicated to my parents, Molly and James,
who brought up their family in a loving and Christian way.

Also to my beloved husband Roni
who has encouraged me all along the way.

To my children Ruth, Suzanna, and James,
who have brought so much joy into my life.

Contents

Acknowledgments | vii

Part One: Approaching Theology

Chapter 1	An Introduction to Christian Theology | 3
Chapter 2	Doing Theology | 13
Chapter 3	Reason and Revelation | 27
Chapter 4	General and Special Revelation | 34

Part Two: Theology in History

Chapter 5	Historical Overview | 45
Chapter 6	The Spread of Gnosticism | 53
Chapter 7	North African Thinkers | 61
Chapter 8	The Controversy of Arianism | 69

Part Three: Knowing God

Chapter 9	The Trinity | 79
Chapter 10	The Doctrine of God | 88
Chapter 11	The Attributes of God | 97

PART FOUR: Jesus, Son of God

CHAPTER 12	The Incarnation of Jesus	115
CHAPTER 13	Walking with Jesus	122
CHAPTER 14	The Death and Resurrection of Jesus	135
CHAPTER 15	Commissioned for Mission	147
CHAPTER 16	Conclusion	156

Appendix | 159

About the Author | 167

Bibliography | 169

Acknowledgments

So many people have contributed to this theological conversation. I am grateful to all those at the Nazarene Theological College in Didsbury, Manchester, who taught me theology and were an encouragement to me to become a lifelong learner. Their godly lives, humor, and constant help and guidance were pivotal in helping me to take that first dive into the ocean of theological learning, which has been an inspiration to me ever since.

I am also indebted to the staff of Ridley Hall, Cambridge, and The Cambridge Federation who continued to teach and guide me in my theological studies and MA in Practical Theology.

I am grateful to the many people to whom I have ministered over the years, in the UK and abroad, who have shared their thoughts and lives with me. My spiritual journey has been a truly cross-cultural and missional one, and this has brought enormous enrichment to my approach to life, my thinking, and my beliefs.

Many thanks to Margie Sherman for her painstaking proofreading of the manuscript and her faithful witness to the Lord.

Thanks to Dr Richard Harvey for suggestions regarding the text of the book.

PART ONE

Approaching Theology

Chapter 1

An Introduction to Christian Theology

THIS CHAPTER WILL INTRODUCE the idea of knowing God and look at the study of theology as well as briefly considering the work of some important Christian thinkers. These include Augustine of Hippo, J.I. Packer, Simone Weil, and Ghanaian theologian Mercy Amba Oduyoye. They are theologians of varying periods in church history who express different points of view. This leads to the discussion of theology as a two-fold activity in which the importance of both the individual and the community is seen in working out the Christian life. We will look at why it is important to root theology in Scripture. We will also deal with the big questions of life and how we work out our faith in daily life.

I have included some study questions at the end of each chapter to help you interact and make your response to what you have read. There is also an appendix at the back to briefly introduce the theologians who are included in this book.

THE STUDY OF GOD

This book aims to deal with the question, 'What is Christian theology?' It is intended for anyone who wants to discover more about their faith, both beginner theological students and those Christians who are keen to learn more and enrich their understanding of God. It may also be of interest to ordained ministers who are continuing to learn, despite their busy lives.

Part One: Approaching Theology

Everybody needs to learn more about theology. Engaging with theology, even at a basic level, will help you to grow in your relationship with Jesus Christ, as well as develop your ability to think critically and analytically about theology, and therefore about God.

I have heard people talk about theology as if it is something to be avoided at all costs. What they do not realize is that we all have an idea of who God is and what he is like. Theology, after all, is simply thoughts and words about God. It would help you to stop for a moment and ask yourself the all-important question, 'How do I view God?' It may help you to write down some keywords or ideas to capture your thoughts about God. You may be a bit hazy about exactly what you do think, although you may feel that he is important to you.

In his book *Knowing God*, J. I. Packer quotes from Spurgeon's 1855 morning sermon about the study of God:

> No subject of contemplation will tend more to humble the mind, than thoughts of God . . . But while the subject *humbles* the mind, it also *expands* it. He who often thinks of God, will have a larger mind than the man who simply plods around this narrow globe . . . The most excellent study for expanding the soul, is the science of Christ, and Him crucified, and the knowledge of the Godhead in the glorious Trinity. Nothing will so enlarge the intellect, nothing so magnify the whole soul of man, as a devout, earnest, continued investigation of the great subject of the Deity. And, whilst humbling and expanding, this subject is eminently consolatory. Oh, there is, in contemplating Christ, a balm for every wound; in musing on the Father, there is a quietus for every grief; and in the influence of the Holy Ghost, there is a balsam for every sore. Would you lose your sorrow? Would you drown your cares? Then go, plunge yourself in the Godhead's deepest sea; be lost in his immensity; and you shall come forth as from a couch of rest, refreshed and invigorated. I know nothing which can so comfort the soul; so calm the swelling billows of sorrow and grief; so speak peace to the winds of trial, as a devout musing upon the subject of the Godhead . . . [1]

The conviction behind Packer's book is that ignorance of God and his ways and the lack of the practice of communion with him contribute to the weakness of the church today. How much more so now that nearly fifty years have passed since his book was written. If we aim to learn about

---

1. Packer, *Knowing God*, 14–15.

An Introduction to Christian Theology

God, then that knowledge cannot be an end in itself. It must lead us to quiet meditation on the things of God, to prayer and to praise. How much better if this occurs in the community of God's people.

Packer continues: "We must learn to measure ourselves, not by our knowledge about God, not by our gifts and responsibilities in the church, but by how we pray and what goes on in our hearts."[2] He further suggests that to know what does go on in our hearts we need to approach God to show us.

The world that we live in is largely ignorant of God and sees him as being distant and uninvolved with our modern age. This includes many Christians who, if asked to talk about God, would find it very difficult. My hope in writing this book is that God would be brought a great deal closer and that we would discover more of his love and grace.

Sometimes people fear that they do not know enough or have not studied like their local minister and therefore would not dream of studying theology. I hope that you will change your thinking and realize that we all have a contribution to make and insights that will help others.

Grenz and Olson sum it up: "First, theology is inescapable for all thinking, reflecting Christians, and the difference between lay theologians and professional theologians is one of degree, not kind. Second, professional theologians and lay theologians (all reflective Christians of whatever profession) need one another."[3]

Jeff Astley explores the question of just who does theology:

> This great resource of experience, including the experience of reflecting on and testing its theology against its experience, is too significant to ignore. If experience is the grounding of theology, should we not try to tap some of this? Academic theologians should be more curious about what ordinary believers have come up with. They should be willing to look and see whether there is some theological *wisdom* out there, often forged through experiences that they may never share – as well as those that they too shall suffer or celebrate.[4]

When visiting other countries and speaking to Christians from cultural backgrounds different from my own, I have found my horizons to be

---

2. Packer, *Knowing God*, 15.
3. Grenz and Olson, *Who Needs Theology?* 13–14.
4. Astley, *Ordinary Theology*, 149.

broadened, and my appreciation for who God is and how he is at work in his world has been deepened.

My time spent in Pakistan among the Marwari Bheel tribes showed me how keen they were to learn more about God. They were very responsive, listening with avid attention to what was being taught to them and soaking up the Word of God like sponges.

When I stayed in the upper north-west of Ghana, I ministered among rural churches that often had no building and simply met under a tree in the equatorial heat, with the people sitting on benches. I taught the Saturday Bible school to prepare the preachers for what they would share on the Sunday morning in their villages, as most of them were not able to read the Bible for themselves.

As I got to know the people, the women told me life was so hard for them that they had been contemplating taking their lives. Then the gospel message was brought to their village and God transformed their lives. This gave them the joy of the Lord, despite their poverty and difficulties. Things began to improve as the whole community was affected by the Christian gospel and change was brought into their neighborhood. I learned a great deal from them, and I had the privilege of sharing the Word of God with eleven rural churches.

Mercy Amba Oduyoye, a Ghanaian theologian, wrote her book *Daughters of Anowa* from a Christian and liberation perspective. She explains that where liberation is needed, there is a root cause that needs to be attended to and eliminated. In its place is the fullness of life that Jesus promised. Her immediate concern is how liberation relates to African women and their place in the church. Her interpretation of this passage from Isaiah is not dealing with the question of people suffering from inherent disabilities, but rather she is addressing the question of the end of women's oppression.[5] She shows how Jesus' reading of Isaiah could apply to our contemporary world:

> The poor will hear good news.
> Those who are depressed will feel the comfort that stimulates action;
> Those who are oppressed will be encouraged and
> enabled to free themselves.
>
> Abilities rather than disabilities will be what counts.
> All who are blind to their own and others' oppression

---

5. Luke 4:18–19, Isaiah 61:1–3.

will come to new insights.

> And God will pardon all at the jubilee.
> It will be a new beginning for all.
> That is liberation.[6]

If you are launching into the study of theology with some trepidation, then you can relax and begin to enjoy the adventure. You will have a great deal to learn, but many people have gone ahead of you and begun the discovery and written down many things that will help to chart the territory in illuminating ways. Perhaps it is a bit like doing scuba diving for the first time. Having got over your nerves about going underwater, you realize that there is a world out there that is beautiful, interesting, and quite unlike the landscape that you have experienced up to now on dry land. It is time to dive in and discover new things and see and experience what you know is under the sea, but which you have never seen for yourself.

In studying theology we learn about the Christian faith and discover more about God at the same time. God is at work in us, changing us and bringing about a transformation of our lives through the indwelling Holy Spirit. God is at work in us individually and corporately, as the believing community. According to the biblical tradition, encountering God is the foundation of our self-identity, and it goes further as God establishes a covenant people.

The early followers of Jesus were well aware of baptism, for the ritual washing was part of the Jewish faith, as a sign of cleansing and initiation for a convert to Judaism. It was widely used by John the Baptiser and by Jesus himself. It is Paul who helps us to understand how baptism came to be understood later, in Romans 6: 3–4, "Know ye not, that so many of us as were baptized into Jesus Christ were baptized into his death? [4] Therefore we are buried with him by baptism into death: that like as Christ was raised up from the dead by the glory of the Father, even so we also should walk in newness of life." *KJV*.

Thus, Paul shows how baptism is seen now as an initiation into the death and resurrection of Jesus and an entrance into sharing his life and becoming part of his kingdom. Sharing the life of Jesus Christ is also a sharing of the glory of God and points us to the hope of freedom from sin, and union with him in a resurrection like his.

---

6. Oduyoye, *Daughters of Anowa*, 4.

Part One: Approaching Theology

THEOLOGY AND THE CHRISTIAN COMMUNITY

Christian community is also essential to our understanding of theology. The liberation from sin and fear into a new life in Christ is also an entrance into a new people in Christ, whose lives have been shaped by the events of the life, death, and resurrection of Christ. The Christian community plays a practical role in the outworking of Christian life and practice in its encounter with Jesus Christ.[7] Members of the community share in the life of Christ and are led by the Spirit of God into a new and deeper relationship with the triune God. This will also make a difference in how they live their lives and how others are treated.

God is making us more like Jesus Christ and he uses our minds and our hearts to do this. He is busy bringing us and all of the creation closer to fulfilling his purposes. This is the exciting aspect of studying theology. As you reflect on God's life in the world, your own life is also transformed as you encounter God.

Even if you start as someone with very little faith, by persevering in your study about God, you will discover that your life is changed as God teaches you more about himself. His presence in your life is a form of knowledge, but it is also a form of communion with him through prayer. This is what is transformative as you share in the life of Christ. John 17:3 gives us the key to enjoying eternal life: "And this is eternal life, that they know you, the only true God, and Jesus Christ whom you have sent." *ESV.*

God has spoken to us through the prophets and the apostles, and most importantly, through his Son Jesus. Reading the Scriptures will guide us to a deeper knowledge of God. Jesus pointed out to the disciple Thomas in John 14:6–7: "I am the way, and the truth, and the life. No one comes to the Father except through me. [7] If you had known me, you would have known my Father also. From now on you do know him and have seen him." *ESV.*

Knowing God requires us to listen to his Word and allow the Holy Spirit to interpret those things which we read to our hearts and lives. As God speaks to us from his Word we need to respond in obedience and in loving response to the love that he shows us. In John's gospel, there are multiple references to how much Jesus loves us and cares for us. He speaks of being the good shepherd who cares for his sheep. We see ourselves led and guided by his loving hand. He is also the bread of life: we are fed and

---

7. Grenz, *Theology for the Community*, 7.

nourished by his life in us. When we are weary and burdened, he comes to us and gives us rest.

GRAPPLING WITH GOD

One of the most influential Christian theologians was Augustine of Hippo (354–430 CE). He was a theologian and philosopher from North Africa and became bishop of Hippo. He was considered one of the most important of the Church Fathers, and his works include his *Confessions, The City of God, The Trinity,* and *On Christian Doctrine.*

In his book *The Trinity*, Augustine reflects on how much we are hindered in our discovery of the reality of God by our narrowness of understanding and pride and sinfulness, that prevent us from enjoying the whole of God's creation. We are obstructed in our ability to connect with the reality of God because of our self-life. On the other hand, a change takes place when God transforms our reality, as he draws us nearer to himself and helps us to acknowledge our weakness.[8]

Simone Weil (1909–1943), the French thinker and theologian, speaks of theological formation as being like an adventure into a labyrinth. This adventure is one of not knowing where you are going, and it can be threatening and even disorientating, but if you keep going you will, at last, discover God at the center, and he is the one who is luring you into where a miraculous change takes place.[9] Weil uses the dramatic analogy of being eaten and digested by God but coming out changed by him and ready to point others to come into the labyrinth.

Such a labyrinth experience was experienced by the disciples of Jesus when he was crucified. They found an empty tomb and then a risen Lord, who loved them despite their betrayal and lack of faith. After the resurrection of Jesus, his disciples began to be transformed in their understanding of who he was and who they were as his followers.

LOOKING AT JESUS

Since we are looking at Christian theology, it makes sense that we will be thinking about Jesus Christ. Yet since, as Christians, we believe in God as

---

8. Augustine, *On the Trinity*, 137.
9. McIntosh, *Divine Teaching*, 17–18.

Part One: Approaching Theology

Father, Son, and Holy Spirit, we will also be viewing God the Father and the Holy Spirit, whom Jesus sent on the day of Pentecost. An important question is why we should learn more about Jesus Christ and who he really is.

In the view of N.T. Wright, "The most basic reason for grappling with the historical question of Jesus is that we are made for God: for God's glory, to worship God and reflect his likeness. That is our heart's deepest desire, the source of our vocation."[10] The New Testament shows us that Jesus has revealed God, and supremely by looking at Jesus do we encounter God made flesh.

REFLECTING ON THE QUESTIONS OF LIFE

The word theology is made up of two Greek words, namely *theos* (God) and *logos* (word). One way of putting it is that theology is God-talk. It is words, ideas, and discourse about God.

Grenz and Olson point out: "Theology is any reflection on the ultimate questions of life that point toward God."[11] Why am I here? Who is God? Who is Jesus? What is the purpose of being on this earth? The answer to the question of 'Why am I here?' has some biblical content but it also has an answer that is unique to each person, for God has a plan and purpose for each one of us. It is this uniqueness that we continue to discover and unfold throughout our lives, which makes it very exciting. We discover the answer through our relationship with Jesus Christ, which grows day by day. It helps us to understand more about the Bible, for this guides us to make Godly decisions as we journey through life.

So, it seems that theology requires a good deal of reflection and thinking on our part, about life and why we are here. We are going to have to grapple with the big questions about the purpose and existence of God. We will need to discover more about why Jesus was born into this world and how he fulfilled the purposes that God had in sending him here. This is often called the study of Christology, which is derived from the word Christ. This is a branch of Christian theology and is important in helping us to understand the New Testament writings.

Plantinga et al. remind us that historic, orthodox Christian theology also has resources for us to address the problems of today's world. We

---

10. Wright, *The Challenge of Jesus*, 3–4.
11. Grenz and Olson, *Who Needs Theology*, 13.

continue with the ongoing task of theology as our faith continues to seek answers and a deeper understanding of a continually changing world.[12]

CREATED TO KNOW GOD

If it seems to you that you are setting out in a storm where debates about God abound and some say, "God is dead" then you are probably right. Yet, as we make our way through some of the theological issues that faced the early church and continued through history, we will see that those Christians also faced storms, but they persevered and paved the way for us in the twenty-first century.

Paul encourages us in Romans 5:1–5 that despite our circumstances we will experience the peace of God.

"Therefore, since we have been justified by faith, we have peace with God through our Lord Jesus Christ. [2] Through him we have also obtained access by faith into this grace in which we stand, and we rejoice in hope of the glory of God. [3] Not only that, but we rejoice in our sufferings, knowing that suffering produces endurance, [4] and endurance produces character, and character produces hope, [5] and hope does not put us to shame, because God's love has been poured into our hearts through the Holy Spirit who has been given to us." *ESV.*

Romans 8:38–39 also encourages us that nothing will separate us from the love of God. "For I am sure that neither death nor life, nor angels nor rulers, nor things present nor things to come, nor powers, [39] nor height nor depth, nor anything else in all creation, will be able to separate us from the love of God in Christ Jesus our Lord." *ESV.*

According to John 17:3, "And this is eternal life, that they know you, the only true God, and Jesus Christ whom you have sent." *ESV.*

We have been created by God to know him. This is the aim in life that we should be headed for. Knowing God is not quite like knowing another human being. We come to know the almighty God when he reveals himself to us. This takes place as we become more acquainted with the Scriptures and Christian truth. We open our hearts to him and develop a relationship with him.

In the course of this book, we will see Jesus as both God and human, and we will examine his relationship with God the Father and the Holy Spirit when we deal with the issue of the Trinity. The history of how we

---

12. Plantinga et al., *Introduction*, 2.

Part One: Approaching Theology

understand this today has been a long and very complex one with the realization that mystery lies at its heart, alongside the revelation of God.

I have sought to introduce the history of theology, some of the interesting theologians both ancient and modern, contributing themes of theology, and the idea of the overarching story contained in Biblical theology. These are all huge topics in their own right, so inevitably my short introduction cannot deal with them all in great depth. Rather they serve as a pointer to whet the appetite of the reader, bringing a realization that there is indeed a large world of scholarship out there that deserves to be explored.

STUDY QUESTIONS

1. Discuss the importance of studying theology?
2. What would you consider the main reasons for the weakness of the church today?
3. In what ways is theology important for the Christian community?
4. How can the study of theology help us to reflect on the questions of life?
5. How can we fulfill the aim in life to know God?

Chapter 2

Doing Theology

DEFINITIONS OF THEOLOGY AND brief introductions to the work of Lesslie Newbigin, John and Charles Wesley, Charles Gerkin, Stanley Hauerwas, and Arthur Pink help us with our exploration of theology. God's story in the Bible and the landscape of faith is introduced and the theme of redemption in the account of the exodus reveals some of God's gracious dealing with his people. A brief discussion on the Bible and the inspiration of Scripture leads to the importance of identifying a core of Christian beliefs in the great tradition.

FAITH SEEKING UNDERSTANDING

One definition of theology is *faith seeking understanding*.[1] This definition goes back at least to the great medieval theologian Anselm of Canterbury. It shows that we do not have to understand everything about the Bible to believe. Faith has to do with our heart, that is the central core of our will and character. It pertains to what we are committed to, and in this case, it is Jesus Christ. As we love and serve him, and read the Bible and hear it expounded regularly, we will begin to understand more about just what it means to be a Christian. It is God himself who draws us to himself and opens our hearts and minds to know and love him.

---

1. Grenz and Olson, *Who Needs Theology*, 16.

Part One: Approaching Theology

THEOLOGY AND PRACTICE

David Ford gives the following definition: "Theology deals with questions of meaning, truth, beauty, and practice raised in regard to religions and pursued through a range of academic disciplines."[2] This definition takes us into a broader understanding of looking at the whole of life and just how our search for God can influence our thinking, our actions, and what decisions we make in life.

This reflecting on life helps us to be able to understand and then articulate what it is that we believe about God and Jesus Christ, and how this will affect how we live our lives for the sake of Jesus and others. We are marshaling our thoughts in the right way to be able to take action and live as we should.

Many people think that reading the Bible is all that is needed. It is good to read the Bible and gain a deep understanding of it. Biblical Studies helps us to understand the Bible better and it often overlaps with Christian theology. Theology is not only doctrine, although it deals with doctrine. Studying theology requires good Biblical knowledge and knowledge of Christian doctrine and teaching. It cannot stop at being theoretical only and must go on to allowing this knowledge to be expressed in action and the transformation of mind and character.

The ancient Athenian scholar Socrates pointed out that the unexamined life is not worth living. We need to examine what we are doing and how we are living and behaving. This responsibility to life and how we live it should spread outwards to the believing community and to the society in which we live. As we live and learn we can become those who can explain the way to others.

INVOLVED IN GOD'S STORY

Although there are competing stories being told today about our universe, the belief in God as creator and redeemer is of great significance. Right from the book of Genesis, at the beginning of the Bible, we are reminded that the biblical stories happened in time with a beginning and an ending, which helps us to locate ourselves in God's story.[3] We are encouraged to undertake the task of theology by becoming involved in God's story. As we

---

2. Ford, *Theology*, 16.
3. Lodahl, *Story of God*, 14–15.

ask, seek, and knock we journey through the biblical story and the story of God's people through history.

The Scriptures are the primary source for our thinking about God. It is a vast collection of Hebrew, some Aramaic, and Greek literature written in different styles and collected over several centuries, and in it, we encounter the story of God. We follow how God acts and how he reveals himself through history. He leads human beings to encounter him and discover his plan for the redemption of the entire created order.

REDEMPTION IN THE EXODUS

We see God at work in saving the people of Israel in the exodus from Egypt and his giving of the Sinai covenant under the leadership of Moses. In both Judaism and Christianity, faith is centered on God's interaction with his people in history. The nature of these stories is rooted in the conviction that God is at work to bring about salvation through these events.

It was Moses, in Exodus 15:6–8, who sang a song about the might of God in saving his people when he stretched out his hand over the sea and God swept back the water so that the Israelites could pass over. This story has been dramatically depicted in film and art to show the miracle of God's deliverance of his people from slavery under the Egyptians and their passing through the Red Sea on dry ground to freedom, and the annihilation of the Egyptian army as the water flooded back.

It is in verses 13 and 17 of this chapter that Moses tells the purpose of God in this great deliverance. He has led the people whom he redeemed, to guide them to his holy habitation, and he will plant them in the mountain of his dwelling which his hand has established. "This declaration by Moses strongly implies that one of the most important goals of God in delivering the Israelites from Egypt through the exodus, was the settlement of Yahweh in the midst of his special people."[4]

CHARLES GERKIN AND STANLEY HAUERWAS

Charles Gerkin and Stanley Hauerwas both argue for the importance of the stories of God's activities in the Bible. Gerkin, as a practical theologian, shows how the stories of the Bible help us to see the world and human life

---

4. Duvall and Hays, *God's Relational Presence*, 29.

within God's plans and purposes and his direction, and that this is situated within that overarching biblical narrative.[5]

For Hauerwas, ethics is important, and he places it in the context of the biblical story. He shows that to understand the world we need to understand the biblical story. For him, it is essential to understand God in a story, and we come to that understanding through the story of Israel and the life of Jesus, that enables us to understand both God and the world in which we live.

Another good reason to understand the big picture is that to preach properly, we need to do so in the context of the unfolding biblical story. In this sense, the Bible is progressive in its revelation. It is also historical and cultural, as well as literary. For every text that is preached, the task that is undertaken is to interpret it in terms of the Scriptural teaching of history as a whole, and the one universal kingdom of God. This reaches back to the creation of the heavens and the earth and reaches forward to the new creation. In preaching, news is announced, and the story is told, which is a real story.

PROPHESIES OF THE MESSIAH

A useful book that provides a selection of God's promises to the Jews and the prophecies of the Messiah that were fulfilled in Jesus Christ, is *The Prophets Speak from the Holy Scriptures*.

The coming of the Messiah is seen in his birth in Isaiah 7:14: "Therefore the Lord himself shall give you a sign; Behold, a virgin shall conceive, and bear a son, and shall call his name Immanuel." *KJV*

Prophecy regarding his family can be found in Isaiah 11:1: "And there shall come forth a rod out of the stem of Jesse, and a Branch shall grow out of his roots." *KJV*

A prophecy about the anointing of Jesus is in Isaiah 11:2: "And the spirit of the LORD shall rest upon him, the spirit of wisdom and understanding, the spirit of counsel and might, the spirit of knowledge and of the fear of the LORD." *KJV*.[6]

---

5. Bartholomew and Goheen, *Drama of Scripture*, 148–149.
6. Arthur, *Prophets Speak*, 45.

Doing Theology

ARTHUR PINK

Arthur Pink (1886–1952), one of the most influential evangelical theologians in the second half of the twentieth century, points out the importance of these prophecies in his book on the attributes of God:

> The perfect knowledge of God is exemplified and illustrated in every prophecy recorded in His Word. In the Old Testament are to be found scores of predictions concerning the history of Israel, which were fulfilled to their minutest detail, centuries after they were made. In them too are scores more foretelling the earthly career of Christ, and they too were accomplished literally and perfectly. Such prophecies could only have been given by One who knew the end from the beginning, and whose knowledge rested upon the unconditional certainty of the accomplishment of everything foretold. In like manner, both Old and New Testament contain many other announcements yet future, and they too "must be fulfilled" (Luke 24:44), must because foretold by Him who decreed them.[7]

THE TOOLS OF THEOLOGY

We probably think of tools as something useful in gardening or agriculture, or even engineering or cooking, depending on our interests in life. Grenz and Olson refer to the tools of theology as the resources that we use for theological construction.[8] We could also view them as the raw materials. Grenz suggests that there are three major sources for theology. These are the Biblical message, the theological heritage of the church, and the historical and cultural context in which we live.[9]

We may wonder whether it is important to bother about having the right resources or even to make use of them at all. We will not be able to do the task of theological study if we don't make use of these resources.

The good chef makes sure to plan to purchase the best and freshest of food. She will also buy the best quality knives and tools for cooking. She will work hard at studying the best ways to make sauces and mix flavors, and she will take time to practice and to do preparation before she comes to cook the food. In the same way, we need to spend time and effort on

---

7. Pink, *Attributes of God*, 17.
8. Grenz and Olson, *Who Needs Theology*, 92.
9. Grenz, *Theology for the Community*, 16.

discovering the message of the Bible and researching our theological and cultural heritage.

WHAT IS THE BIBLE?

When it comes to beliefs, we often live with the misconception that beliefs are just 'there.' Perhaps we are inclined to say, 'All we need is the Bible.' This is a good time to think through exactly what the Bible is.

Grenz and Olson suggest seven things that the Bible is not. It is not a long list of beliefs, although it does contain beliefs that we can draw out of it. Neither is it a written exposition on theology, although it contains many aspects of theology. It is not a series of long explanations about theories and ideas on church teachings, called doctrine, although doctrines are taken from it. It is not a summary of what God's people believe. It is not a history textbook, although it covers history from its beginning to its end. Neither is it a science textbook or a moral code.

On the other hand, the Bible helps us to understand God and how he deals with his creation. It gives us an insight into who God is and what he is doing. It is a lengthy and fascinating book written over a long time and containing narratives, poetry, proverbs, history, laws, and instructions to specific people. The Bible has been understood as one unfolding story, which includes in it the acts of God in history. It is written in several different genres by many different authors. It is important to see in this text the theological reality to which it bears witness and to spend time reflecting on its unfolding story.[10]

THE INSPIRATION OF SCRIPTURE

One of the important things to bear in mind is that the Bible is both human and divine. Therefore, we need to consider just how we go about reading the Bible. Perhaps you might like to reflect upon what you understand by the inspiration of Scripture before you read on.

There are many different answers to this question, which is what makes it a fascinating subject to think about. It is vital to our understanding of the value of the Bible. Lodahl argues that inspiration does not mean word for word dictation from God to the Biblical writer. It most strongly indicates

---

10. Grenz and Olson, *Who Needs Theology*, 89.

the living presence of God's Spirit (Greek – *pneuma*: breath, air in motion) that offers divine insight into the writer's real humanity.[11] As Christians, we believe that the biblical interpretations of history are inspired, and the writers of Scripture were given divine inspiration and insight to interpret God's purposes in world events and history.

In Israel's history the prophets were inspired by God to the extent that they were able to write, 'Thus says the LORD.' In the early church, it was the apostles who were inspired by the Holy Spirit to write the gospel accounts and letters, which reveal to us the four-fold account of the life of Jesus Christ, his death and resurrection, and the spread of the gospel in the early church.

What we understand by the inspiration of Scripture will have implications on how we read the Bible and how this affects our faith and the way we live our lives. There are times when the vision of who God is and what he is doing lies beneath the surface. This is often illustrated rather than clearly stated. The Bible does not lay out its teaching in the same kind of systematic way in which the church creeds set it out.

We may find it frustrating at times that the Bible does not answer every question that we have. It is silent on many issues that face our world today and have done throughout history. As we look back over history, we see the need for fresh evaluations of life and the need to apply Scripture to issues we face. We will not find a clear chronological record of things or an explanation of the nature of the universe in the Bible. Having said that, the Bible is a very long story of the activity of God for the salvation of the world.[12]

FAITH IS A RELATIONAL MATTER

The relevance of Christian theology is that it emphasizes that faith is a *relational* matter.[13] Faith has to do with our relationship with God and trusting him. In his book *Holiness in the Gospels*, Kent Brower argues that the gospel of Mark shows human holiness always in relationship to the God who is holy. The disciples not only identified with Jesus, but they were in an ongoing relationship with him, and this began with a call to follow Jesus.

---

11. Lodahl, *Story of God*, 22–23.
12. Bartholomew and Goheen, *Drama of Scripture*, ix.
13. McGrath, *Mere Theology*, 3.

Part One: Approaching Theology

The same is true of us living today, for discipleship is the answering of that call. It is important to note that discipleship is not for individuals alone but is a communal calling. It is worked out with Jesus on his mission, for disciples are called both to proclaim and to live out the kingdom of God. Discipleship is a journey that requires a commitment to Jesus daily. He leads us through life even when we are not sure of where we are headed. Because Jesus enables us, our journey should be one of growth and development, even if at times we may fail him. He offers his forgiveness and restoration to us, for his grace is always ongoing.[14]

While we may have a longing to understand more about God, there should also be a transformative impact on our lives. This will affect our relationships with others around us. Theological reflection will help to deepen our faith and enrich our personal lives. It also helps us to work out our faith in very practical ways in the real world.

Duvall and Hays argue that the central theme of the Bible is God's relational presence which weaves its way through each book of the Bible.

> ... [I]n arguing that the relational presence of God is the cohesive center of biblical theology, we are neither ignoring nor downplaying the importance of other prevalent and highly significant biblical themes (e.g., covenant, the kingdom of God), but rather suggesting that the central megatheme of God's relational presence connects all of these other themes into the big overarching plot of the biblical story.[15]

This cohesive center of God's relational presence is what "drives the plot of the story from beginning to end."[16] Duvall and Hays show that all the themes in Biblical theology depend on this center for their structure and cohesion, even if this association is complex both historically and theologically.

You may have come across people who criticize theology and think it is a waste of time in our modern life. They may also think that we are trying to run away from the realities of life by engaging with theology. Rather it is a tool to help us, as Christians, to take action in an informed way, with the help of those who have gone before us and themselves reflected on the same kind of life issues that face us today.

---

14. Brower, *Holiness*, 99–101.
15. Duvall and Hays, *God's Relational Presence*, 5.
16. Duvall and Hays, *God's Relational Presence*, 5.

Doing Theology

ESSENTIAL CHRISTIAN BELIEFS

You may be aware that people have different ideas about the Bible and how to interpret it, and this can create anxiety and even division and conflict.

Olson argues that not all Christians believe exactly alike in everything.[17] Yet Christian thinkers and leaders have recognized the importance of identifying a core of essential Christian beliefs that followers of Jesus can affirm to be considered Christian. Even in the first epistle of John in the New Testament, the writer speaks of the importance of believing that Christ came in the flesh.

1 John 4:2-3: "By this you know the Spirit of God: every spirit that confesses that Jesus Christ has come in the flesh is from God, ³ and every spirit that does not confess Jesus is not from God. And this is the spirit of the antichrist, of which you have heard that it is coming; and now it is already in the world." *NRSV.*

Jesus, the Son of the Father, who has eternally existed, became flesh by taking on human form. This miraculous event was that Jesus, the Word of God through whom the universe was made out of nothing, became a human being. We call this the incarnation and will look at this later in the book.

Here we see a clear separation between biblical beliefs and those ideas that are incompatible with the Christian faith and do not have their source in God. For Christianity, beliefs do matter, but some beliefs are secondary and do not form the very central ideas of what is important to the foundation of Christianity.

THE GREAT TRADITION

Christian theologians down the years have had to define those things that are authentically Christian and which beliefs are included in what has become known as the 'great tradition.' This great tradition has stretched down through history from the second century until the present time.

Our cultural background and traditions provide the lens through which we understand the Bible and what is important in the tradition. There are no absolute answers to what it includes, and it has been debated at great length by different denominational groups. Christian theologians have found sufficient common ground regarding what it means to be a

17. Olson, *Mosaic*, 34–35.

Christian. Three main streams are Roman Catholicism, Orthodoxy, (Greek and Russian) and Protestantism.

Much of what is included in this great tradition was taken from the early church fathers and the Reformers. The great Reformation theologian Martin Luther held to *sola scriptura* (Scripture alone as the source for faith and practice) and the ecumenical councils of the undivided church, namely Nicaea, Constantinople, Ephesus, and Chalcedon.

Reason and tradition are also major sources for theology. Tradition comes from the Latin word *traditio,* meaning that which is 'handed down' or 'handed on.' Paul handed down the Christian teaching to others, as we read in 1 and 2 Timothy and Titus.

1 Tim. 1:18: "I am giving you these instructions, Timothy, my child, in accordance with the prophecies made earlier about you, so that by following them you may fight the good fight." *NRSV.*

THE QUADRILATERAL

Although there is no uniform agreement about the sources and norms of the Christian faith, there is a consensus that has developed through time that there are four main sources used by Christian theologians that have come to be known as the 'Wesleyan Quadrilateral' or simply the Quadrilateral. These norms are Scripture, tradition, reason, and experience. They are not unique to John Wesley, the founder of the Methodist movement and great preacher of the eighteenth century, as they predate him. Many Christian thinkers from the second century church up to the present day have used these to guide and determine sound doctrine.

By *Scripture,* the church fathers and the Reformers would mean the written form of divine revelation found in the canon of the Bible. There has been some disagreement about the inclusion or exclusion of the Apocrypha, but there is general agreement about the authority of the Bible to shape correct Christian belief. *Tradition* would refer to the beliefs held in common by Christians from the time of the early church fathers, including the ecumenical creeds and the Reformation confessions of faith. *Reason* would refer to the search for logic, coherence, and what is intelligible. *Experience* does not refer to private, personal experience, but rather the religious experience of God's people in the community of faith.[18]

---

18. Olson, *Mosaic,* 55–56.

Doing Theology

We need to strive for a deeper understanding of the Christian faith, as it has the power to move us spiritually, but also to capture our imagination and persuade our minds of the depths of the reality of the gospel. There is also an intellectual core to the Christian faith. "We cannot love God without wanting to understand more about Him. We are called to love God with our minds, as well as our hearts and souls (Matthew 22:37)."[19]

LANDSCAPE OF FAITH

McGrath uses the metaphor of the landscape of faith to describe how our faith can be likened to the experience of standing in a beautiful scenic spot, which may be quite difficult to describe to a friend. You may not be able to draw an exact representation of what you see. You could perhaps draw a sketch map to include aspects such as woods, mountains, streams, and villages. Theology is like this type of map, which helps to describe what we encounter through faith. It will help us to "articulate, deepen and communicate the Christian vision of God in all its fullness and wonder."[20]

What we see and understand is even more helpfully done in community. A group will see more than an individual, and a corporate view will not only see more but more accurately as well. That is why we need the body of Christ to build up a full understanding of the gospel.

The early church had relationships with the wider community, and God was at work in their midst by the power of the Holy Spirit in bringing new people to enjoy this fellowship and the real sense of community and loving relationships. Acts 2:47: "Praising God and having favor with all the people. And the Lord added to the church daily such as should be saved." KJV

LESSLIE NEWBIGIN

Lesslie Newbigin (1909–1998) was a British theologian, missionary, and Bishop in the Church of South India. In his later years, he lectured on mission and was one of the most well-respected theologians of the twentieth century. He took up the theme of the church and its role in the community.

---

19. McGrath, *Mere Theology*, 5.
20. McGrath, *Mere Theology*, 6.

> The only hermeneutic of the Gospel is a congregation of men and women who believe it and live by it. The church is to be the primary agent of mission and if it does not exhibit evident community and transformed lives then any number of evangelistic events and church projects will have limited credibility.[21]

Newbigin speaks of history moving towards a goal that is distinctive in the Hebrew understanding of history. The Hebrew Scriptures look forward to a consummation of history. This is not reached by the forces within it, for all human existence is a gift of God and the development of history is his promise.[22]

Theology also values the views of those who have mapped and traveled the road of faith in the past. We have people such as Augustine of Hippo, Thomas Aquinas, Martin Luther, and Karl Barth, who are all dead now but are considered today to be authoritative voices who can enrich our thinking and challenge us to think through issues ourselves. They are part of the great tradition, which is a treasure of insights and learning that we make use of today.

The Bible is central to the theological debate and personal faith. Weaving all the biblical threads together in the Christian understanding of Jesus produces a rich tapestry. He is interpreted as a healer and prophet. But the New Testament also portrays him as a human being who became hungry and thirsty, who suffered and died. He is also our Savior. The Christian church came to the understanding that he was truly God and truly human. The Trinity is also found in this weaving, as Jesus is part of the Trinity.

WESLEY HOLINESS

In the eighteenth century, John and Charles Wesley contributed to the great revival of the Christian faith in England. For Wesley, Scriptural holiness was summed up in the love of God and of our neighbors, which lay at the heart of the teachings of Jesus himself.

Wesley wrote, "Christian perfection . . . is nothing higher and nothing lower than this: the pure love of God and man — the loving God with all our heart and soul and our neighbour as ourselves. It is governing the heart

---

21. Newbigin, *Gospel*, 227.
22. Newbigin, *Gospel*, 103.

and life, running through all our tempers [emotions], words and actions. I ask no more. I am interested in no other sort of perfection or holiness." [23]

We can reflect on God's activity shown in Scripture. The church has to do justice to the profound witness to God as found in the Bible, even if it is sometimes difficult to understand. This activity of God is a transforming one, which is rooted in the biblical truth that God is love. Lodahl points out that the contribution the Wesleyan tradition has made to the Christian faith can be summarized by three main aspects of the love of God, and neighbor, and holiness.

First, holiness is *personal* or *experiential*. We are persons standing in relationship to God and others, and we experience the love of God when the Holy Spirit impresses that love into our deepest selves.

Second, holiness is *loving*. For Wesley, the highest human goal is to be immersed in the love of God.

Third, holiness is *expansive*. By this, he means that there is a welcome and embracing of those with differing traditions in the Christian faith. It was this outward-looking approach that led John Wesley to see the whole world as his parish.[24]

Lodahl points out that Wesley had a vision of the love of God for all people and this helped him to seek common ground with Christian people whose worship was quite unlike his own where he could find common ground in the love of God. He often disclosed in his journal that Roman Catholics routinely came to hear him preaching and he wrote a tract or letter 'to a Roman Catholic.'

> Wesley's understanding of holiness, then, encourages a Christian faith that is catholic or universal, rather than narrow and exclusivist, in its attitude towards other traditions. Wesleyan tradition at its best is profoundly open to learn and benefit from others, and to share its insights and particular accents with others. If historically and sociologically the tendency (temptation?) for religious traditions is to isolate themselves in robes of self-righteousness or superiority, the Wesleyan tradition has — and should nurture — a built-in expansive openness to other Christian traditions.[25]

---

23. Lodahl, *Story of God*, 27.
24. Lodahl, *Story of God*, 27–29.
25. Lodahl, *Story of God*, 30.

Part One: Approaching Theology
STUDY QUESTIONS

1. What do you understand by the definition of theology as 'faith seeking understanding?'
2. In what way is Socrates' maxim 'the unexamined life is not worth living' true for the study of theology?
3. In what way does our study of theology help us to be involved in God's story?
4. What do you understand of redemption in the exodus?
5. What can you learn about God's activities in the Bible from Charles Gherkin and Stanley Hauerwas?
6. What do you understand by the tools of theology?
7. How important is the way in which we understand the inspiration of Scripture?
8. 'Faith is a relational matter.' What do you understand by this concept?
9. How have essential Christian beliefs been defined?

Chapter 3

Reason and Revelation

IN THIS CHAPTER, WE introduce the theology of Thomas Aquinas and some of the Enlightenment philosophies. The concept of revelation is introduced and Luther's idea of the 'God who speaks' is pursued along with the idea of Biblical narrative.

DESCRIBING GOD

Many people, if asked to describe God, would probably describe the figure painted by Michelangelo on the ceiling of the Sistine Chapel or *The Ancient of Days* painted by William Blake. The human figure in the sun sends shafts of light into the dark clouds of chaos, holding in his left hand what appears to be a pair of compasses as if to measure out the universe he is about to create. Keith Ward points out that, although this is a popular graphic for the cover of books about God, Blake was not meaning to portray the "true and living God, but the pseudo-God of Newton, of the machine."[1]

THE RISE OF ENLIGHTENMENT PHILOSOPHIES

This mechanistic approach to nature has its roots in the natural theology of Thomas Aquinas (1224–1274 CE), who emphasized the priority of reason and rationality to support orthodox theism, but at the same time taught that scientific knowledge and religious faith belonged in two different spheres.[2]

---

1. Ward, *God*, 11.
2. Blanchard, *Does God Believe in Atheists?* 41-42.

Part One: Approaching Theology

By the fourteenth century CE, Aquinas's distinction between these two spheres had widened into a dualism that separated reason and faith. This directly influenced the ideas of the Renaissance, which took place over the next three hundred years, the effects of which are still felt today. Movements such as Naturalism, Pantheism, Scepticism, Cartesianism, and Deism were among the Enlightenment philosophies that arose between 1720–1780.

WHAT IS A DEIST?

The American philosopher Norman Geisler defines a deist as someone who "believes that God made the world but does not 'monkey' with it."[3] Deism taught that the designer God is now distant. Deists believe that humankind is capable of attaining the truth, including religious truth, as natural religion based on reason. The result of this way of thinking is that there is no need for revelation or revealed religion. For the religious rationalists, reason became the basis of Enlightenment thought. The logical result of these ideas was that people could not have a direct and personal relationship with their Maker.

For me, this position is untenable, and therefore I suggest that God has revealed himself and continues to do so, and that revelation plays an important part in our knowledge of God, both by general and special revelation. I also think that God reveals himself through self-revelatory acts in history by word and deed.

THE QUESTION OF REVELATION

Ward argues that most, if not all, religions depend not only on reflection but primarily on revelation.[4] Spiritual insight comes through the authoritative guidance of a person or persons to whom God has given some revelation of his divine nature and purpose. This revelation has been given at a particular time and place.

God's story gets told over a long period with "many tellers, twists and complications, and with a rather unobtrusive main Character who does

---

3. Geisler, *Christian Apologetics*, 171.
4. Ward, *God*, 237–238.

not seem to be overly concerned that we get the Story "just right" in every detail."[5]

This fact has produced disagreements among believers in the story and makes the task of unravelling and making sense of the biblical story complicated. However, the biblical writers share the basic premise that God acts in human history to bring about his saving purposes, revealing himself to bring people into a saving relationship with himself and ultimately to redeem the entire created order.

Writers such as F. Gerald Downing, James Barr, and Christopher Evans have written in highly critical terms about the relevance of revelation, questioning whether both the Old and the New Testament ever clearly and explicitly say that God has revealed himself. To answer these objections, we need to answer the questions 'What is revelation?', 'What does the Bible teach on revelation?' and 'How does God reveal himself?'[6]

According to The Shorter Oxford English Dictionary, revelation means "The disclosure of knowledge to man by a divine or supernatural agency" and "Something disclosed or made known by divine or supernatural means."[7] The word disclosure implies that this is knowledge that comes to us from outside ourselves and is beyond our ability to discover. The English word revelation comes from the Latin *revelare*. This is a translation of the Greek *apokalyptein*, which means "to uncover or unveil."[8]

A revelation is a divine act in which the triune God brings into view what has been hidden. The human response to this communication from God is faith. This is known as special revelation and is seen in God's redemptive acts and words in history, and in particular through the Word who became flesh in Jesus Christ.

If divine revelation is denied, there are many other kinds of revelation from many directions in our world, including the principalities and powers of Marxism, fascism, political correctness, and the influence of the media which will come rushing in. We also live with a flood of disinformation from fake news, which desensitizes people to the truth. These are all imitations of the truth, and they bring destruction instead of life. What we are looking for is the revelation of God that will bring his grace and truth to turn back the crisis of meaning that is facing our world.

5. Lodahl, *Story of God*, 16–17.
6. Morris, *I Believe in Revelation*, 16.
7. Morris, *I Believe in Revelation*, 9.
8. Plantinga et al., *Introduction to Christian Theology*, 51.

Part One: Approaching Theology

There are several expressions of revelation in the Synoptic gospels and many in John's gospel. The first is the baptism of Jesus in which all three members of the Trinity are involved. The focus is on Jesus, for it is onto him that the Holy Spirit descends and of him that the Father speaks: "You are my beloved Son . . ." (Mark 1:11). These words are a revelation by God the Father about who Jesus is.

Another example is when Jesus and the disciples were at Caesarea Philippi and discussing who people thought he was. In conclusion to this Jesus asks in Matthew 16:15 who they think he is? Simon Peter answers that he is the Christ, the Son of the living God. Jesus responds to Peter and explains that he is blessed because the Father in heaven has revealed this to him. Yet this revelation of who Jesus is needs some explanation, and when Jesus tells of his forthcoming suffering and death, Peter finds this difficult to understand. This holds revelations of the cross and the resurrection, but they are also revelations of the glory of Jesus as Son of God.

THE GOD WHO SPEAKS

For most Christians, revelation is fundamental to their faith. In Genesis, we are confronted with the God who speaks, and we find him speaking throughout the Bible. Luther's passion was that the Scripture had its own voice. In his *Theology of the Old Testament* Walter Brueggemann, an American theologian picks up Luther's idea of the Bible as a voice of revelation. "This "voice of the Bible" speaks its truth and makes its claim in its own categories, categories that are recurringly odd and unaccommodating. The substance of that truth is God, the Creator of heaven and earth, the God known decisively and uniquely in Jesus of Nazareth."[9]

Brueggemann argues that the Bible is to be understood 'as Scripture' and this is a community activity as people gather and respond, "to the claim that here God is decisively disclosed."[10] By studying the Bible we can begin to understand and receive the revelation of God. John Calvin, a great Reformation theologian, in his *Institutes of the Christian Religion*, encouraged the faithful reading of the Scriptures regarding every aspect of life, thus letting the Bible have its own voice.

---

9. Brueggemann, *Theology of the Old Testament*, 3.
10. Brueggemann, *Theology of the Old Testament*, 3.

NARRATIVE THEOLOGY

Narrative was a recurring subject in the theology of the late twentieth century. As a literary form, there is the presence of a story and a storyteller. These could include history and reported news, and depend on the vision of the narrator, who gives the story coherence, meaning, and direction. A plot with characters and events moves "over time and space through conflict towards resolution."[11]

Scripture is full of narratives, including those of Jesus' life, death, and resurrection. Fackre suggests that the Bible as a book has an 'overarching story' which is no fictive account but a good news story of events that have taken place and also will take place. It is good news about events that have a meaningful significance in the narration, that teaches us and reveals the triune God to us.

THE BIBLICAL MACRO-NARRATIVE

Christian doctrines that have been developed in systematic theology can be understood as chapters in the biblical macro-narrative: the account of creation, the story of the children of Israel, the story of Jesus, and the beginning of the church. Through all of this is woven the centrality of the salvation motif, ending finally with the consummation of all things, with God as the central character who involves himself with humankind.

UNFOLDING DRAMA OF DIVINE DEEDS

As modernity and postmodern theology eclipsed the idea of a biblical narrative, so there has been a resurgence of ecumenical, evangelical, catholic, and postliberal voices speaking once more of the biblical tale and providing an interpretive framework to articulate our knowledge of God.

Narrative is here related to theological form, identifying the pattern of God's actions among us that can be seen as the unfolding of a drama of divine deeds. This biblical story that runs from Genesis to Revelation has Jesus as its center point. The narrative can also provide a framework to discuss the question of revelation. William Abraham comments on historic controversies regarding God's revelation of himself.

---

11. Fackre, *Doctrine of Revelation*, 2–3.

> Divine revelation must not be approached in independence from delineating the divine activity through which God reveals himself. To pick out any one act or activity as the essence of revelation is to miss the total picture, yet this is what has happened in the history of the doctrine of revelation.[12]

Abraham argues that different generations have focussed on different aspects to provide revelation, such as the creation, the prophets and apostles, Jesus Christ, eschatology, and the end of history.

The tendency has been to focus on one of these revelatory acts of God, while they are all integral parts of the great narrative of disclosure, each one a phase in the unfolding story of revelation. I think that the triune God, Father, Son, and Holy Spirit, cannot be seen as a phase in the story of revelation. God underpins the total unfolding story. Each of the perspectives noted above needs to be adopted in our theological view, as all are necessary if we are to have a complete biblical revelation of God.

THE CANONICAL SCRIPTURES

Nearly all Christian thinkers throughout history have considered the canonical Scriptures to be one major norm for deciding on proper Christian belief.[13] When Christians disagree about the meaning of the Bible then there are other norms and sources that come into play, such as tradition, reason, and experience.

Eastern Orthodox and Roman Catholic Christian thinkers have included tradition as a means of revelation, with Scripture as one part of that. Tradition is the agreement of Christians, particularly leaders such as bishops and teachers of the church during the early centuries of Christianity. Which parts of the Bible were selected to be included in the canon was a divinely guided process. Those beliefs and practices that are taught which are not in the Bible but that do not conflict with it, are said by the Orthodox to be part of the tradition. Roman Catholic Christians appeal to Scripture and tradition together. Protestants have looked to the Bible and the Holy Spirit who inspired it and illumines its meaning to believers as the authority for Christian belief. In addition to this, the creeds and creedal statements of the tradition are also considered authoritative.

---

12. Abraham, *Divine Inspiration*, 8.
13. Olson, *Mosaic*, 50.

STUDY QUESTIONS

1. What do you understand by deism?
2. Explain what narrative theology is?
3. What is the importance of the canonical Scriptures?
4. What is the origin of the English word 'revelation?'
5. How has God spoken?

Chapter 4

General and Special Revelation

TRADITIONALLY, CHRISTIANS HAVE SPOKEN of 'general' and 'special' revelation. General revelation is made generally to all people and is not a revelation to a specific nation. It refers to the revelation that is found in nature and human beings. Special revelation refers to the revelation found in Jesus and the Bible. This chapter looks at the idea of general and special revelation and Aquinas' five ways.

GENERAL REVELATION

Revelation in nature is seen in the words of Psalm 19:1, "The heavens declare the glory of God; and the firmament sheweth his handywork." *KJV.* Yet the Psalmist is part of a specific community called by God. In subsequent verses, he tells of creation as speaking, although without speech or words. (Psalm 19:3).

In the book of Romans Paul also speaks of God's invisible nature, namely his eternal power and deity, clearly perceived in the things that have been made.[1] A divine imprint has been left in creation, revealing something of God to humankind. This is also true of humans, whom God made in his own image.[2] Some Christians have argued that it is necessary to develop a natural theology based on the revelation of God in nature and have subordinated the place of the Bible in revelation. The problem with this view is that it depends more on people's apprehension of God in nature, and some may perceive it while others do not. The limitation of this kind

1. Romans 1:20
2. Genesis 1:26

of revelation is that it is of an impersonal kind and is not conducive to developing a relationship of faith and love towards God.

The essence of revelation is that it comes from God and transcends what humans can know by themselves. We cannot by unaided reason know about God's existence and his nature that accords with God's revelation through the Scriptures. Any natural knowledge of God would be vague and not deal with the issue of sin and redemption.

THOMAS AQUINAS (C.1225-1274)

Thomas Aquinas, the great medieval Catholic thinker, believed that humankind could identify pointers to the existence of God drawn from the general human experience of the world. "What we observe in the world— for example, its signs of ordering — can be explained on the basis of the existence of God as its creator ... God has brought the world into existence and impressed the divine image and likeness upon it."[3]

AQUINAS'S FIVE WAYS

Aquinas argued there are five ways that can demonstrate God's existence through general revelation. The first four ways are known as the cosmological argument, based on the origin of things in the world. As we observe things in the world that exist, we find ourselves asking questions regarding their origin, their cause, and what set them in motion. The conclusion we must reach is that there is a Prime Mover who is God. The fifth way of Aquinas is based on the purpose or *telos* of things in the world. This is known as the *teleological argument*. There are order and purpose in the world that also point to the intelligent design that governs the world, and that is God himself.

Aquinas's arguments, which are based on the existence and order of the world and human conscience, only go some way towards a belief in a creator of the world, and a leap of faith is still needed. Such knowledge of God is insufficient for salvation.

---

3. McGrath, *Christian Theology*, 160.

PART ONE: APPROACHING THEOLOGY

KNOWLEDGE OF GOD THROUGH NATURE

John Calvin, (1509–1564) the great Protestant reformer, theologian, and pastor, used Aquinas's belief in a general revelation of God and argued in his work *Institutes of the Christian Religion* that "were it not for sin clouding humans' minds, the revelation of God in nature would yield a true knowledge of God."[4]

Martin Luther, (1483–1546) the German professor of theology, composer, priest, monk, and important figure in the Protestant Reformation, believed and taught that all people have some knowledge of God's existence through nature.

The early church fathers also assumed such a view of a revelation of God, while also seeing that it is inadequate for redemption. The Reformers accepted general revelation, but they rejected natural theology. While God discloses himself in creation, yet sinful humankind is not able to know God through this general revelation.

SPECIAL REVELATION

This formed the basis for the emphasis of the Reformers on special revelation. They taught that God's self-disclosure was necessary both for our salvation and for us to see the revelation that is present in creation. Humans cannot know God until he reveals himself. In Job 11:7, Zophar asks whether you can claim to grasp the mystery of God. Karl Barth, the neo-orthodox theologian, wanted to recover a theology of the Word of God. He would have given a resounding 'No' to Zophar's question.

BARTH'S THEOLOGY OF REVELATION

Barth is known for his theology of revelation. "The Bible is the concrete means by which the Church recollects God's past revelation, is called to expectation of His future revelation, and is thus summoned and guided to proclamation and empowered for it."[5]

For Barth, Jesus makes himself known as the mediator between God and humankind, and as "the One who restores fellowship between them

---

4. Olson, *Mosaic*, 75.
5. Barth, *Church Dogmatics*, 1/1:4, 108.

and accomplishes the justification and sanctification of man."[6] Barth is known for his *dynamic* understanding of revelation where the Word of God is a *happening* and not a thing, and the Bible becomes the Word of God through the work of the Spirit. In *Church Dogmatics*, Barth writes of God's speaking in Jesus Christ as the foundation of Christian theology. God's speaking makes it possible for us to speak about him.

THE REVELATION OF GOD IN SCRIPTURE

Special revelation is used to describe the revelation recorded in Scripture, whereby God has revealed himself, and the way he has done so. Humankind's knowledge of God has come from God himself. James Dunn writes that God has made himself and his will known through his chosen people Israel. "This concept of 'revelation' runs consistently through both testaments of the Christian Bible. So, we can speak quite properly of 'biblical' concepts of revelation."[7]

Dunn discusses revelation through history as God showing himself as the God who acts. This is seen, for example, in the narrative of the exodus from Egypt and his care for his people in the wilderness.

In the New Testament, the revelatory significance of Jesus' death and resurrection is Jesus' 'exodus.' From a Christian perspective, the revelation of Christ is the climax of all previous revelation and the key to making sense of it.

In the account of the transfiguration of Jesus, he is speaking to Moses and Elijah. Luke 9:30–31: "Suddenly they saw two men, Moses and Elijah, talking to him. They appeared in glory and were speaking of his departure, which he was about to accomplish at Jerusalem." *NRSV*

In speaking to Moses and Elijah, who represent the law and the prophets, Jesus unveils the meaning of earlier scriptures. He also reveals the character and purpose of God in his creation and the future unfolding of his death on the cross and resurrection, that he is to accomplish in Jerusalem. He reveals the glory of the invisible God and speaks of the greatest mystery of all, things that the prophets longed to look into.[8]

---

6. Fackre, *Doctrine of Revelation*, 122–123.
7. Avis, *Divine Revelation*, 1.
8. Avis, *Divine Revelation*, 17, 21.

Part One: Approaching Theology

GOD SPEAKS IN HIS WORD AND HIS SON

Without the revelation that Jesus Christ brings, the task of theology would be impossible. God has spoken to us in his Word and through his Son. The Word of God can be understood in two distinct and related senses. In one sense it may be the texts that we have in the Bible, the sourcebook of Christian teaching. In another sense, it applies to Jesus, who is the fulfillment of Biblical teaching and the focus of the Christian faith.

Luther acknowledged that while God might be known through nature, this was limited and inadequate knowledge of God and needed to be supplemented in the light of Scripture. Christ alone is the means, the life, and the mirror through which we see God and know his will."[9]

J. I. Packer reinforces this idea in his discussion on revelation and authority, in which he shows that as God has acted to make known his mind and will, this divine revelation has authority for our lives. The biblical picture of God's servants all through the Bible is of people who both know what God has told them and are living by that knowledge.[10]

Knowing God depends on our listening to his Word and allowing the Holy Spirit to apply it to our lives. As we get to know the Bible better, we will also grow in our knowledge of the nature and character of God and come to appreciate the love he has for us. God deals with us in a personal way, and this is key to getting to know him better as we spend time in his company and discover that he knows us as a friend and that he watches over us.[11]

It is in Jesus that we come to know God. We need to understand him in his context in history as a man appointed by God, as well as God's Word that became flesh, placing the accent on Jesus' deity. Jesus, in his incarnation, both revealed God and embodied knowledge of God. In John's gospel, Jesus spoke of this close relationship with his heavenly Father.

John 5:19–20: Jesus gave them this answer: 'Very truly I tell you, the Son can do nothing by himself; he can do only what he sees his Father doing, because whatever the Father does the Son also does. [20] For the Father loves the Son and shows him all he does. Yes, and he will show him even greater works than these so that you will be amazed.' *NIV.*

---

9. McGrath, *Christian Theology Reader*, 55.
10. Packer, *Knowing Christianity*, 15.
11. Packer, *Knowing Christianity*, 45.

General and Special Revelation

In Jesus, the Way, the Truth, and the Life lies access to God the Father, and in his being is the revelation of God, which he mediates. It is in the God-man Jesus Christ, that the culmination of God's self-communication is seen in creation and history.

DIFFERING IDEAS ABOUT REVELATION

Some call themselves Christians and yet have challenged the Christian consensus that God is specially revealed in Jesus Christ and in Scripture, which is proclaimed and testified by the people of God.

The Eastern Orthodox Church would also want to include the Great Tradition of worship or liturgy to be included in this divine revelation. Most of the Pentecostal groups and charismatics wish to include the ongoing work of the Holy Spirit as testifying to Jesus Christ and still guiding Christians into all truth.[12]

There have been people in history such as Marcion who have had differing ideas about divine revelation and whose thinking has been rejected by Christians in general. Some have gone way beyond special revelation and said that new revelation may rise and supplant this special revelation through Jesus Christ and the Scriptures. The danger of including these teachings as revelation is that they may replace divine revelation.

A DISTORTION OF THE CHRISTIAN FAITH

An example of this took place in the 1930s when the Nazis replaced the confessing church with German culture and Hitler and his party. They were distorting the Christian faith and making Christianity bow the knee to their National Socialism. People like Dietrich Bonhoeffer (1906–1945) and Martin Niemöller (1892–1984) of the Confessing Church stood against this theological aberration. Bonhoeffer paid with his life and Niemöller was incarcerated in concentration camps for the last seven years of Nazi rule, for opposing Hitler and the Nazi ideology. The Barmen Declaration was adopted in 1934 by Christians in the Confessing Church movement, which opposed any belief in a new savior and lord, such as that of the so-called German Christian movement of the Nazis.

---

12. Olson, *Mosaic*, 77.

Another example is that of the Unification Church of the United States, founded by the Rev Sun Myung Moon of Korea, which believes that there will arise out of Asia a new and more complete revelation and salvation than that of Jesus Christ. The book produced by the so-called 'Moonies,' *The Divine Principle,* is believed by them to surpass the revelation of the canonical Bible.

Others have asserted that general, universal revelation that comes through universal reason and is apart from faith, is greater than divine revelation. The German philosopher G.W. F. Hegel (1770–1831) believed that the best of human thought and culture, without any supernatural aid, is divine revelation. For him, all reality is capable of being expressed in rational categories. Jesus Christ is a representation of rational truth that is timeless and universal — the union of God and humanity. Hegel taught that all religions have their valid apprehensions of the 'Real' which is God or the divine.[13]

In contrast to Hegel's rationalism, there has also been the idea of divine revelation as being interior and mystical. In this case, Christians would reject an objective divine revelation and rely on their inner interpretation that listens for God to speak personally to them. Teachers such as Rudolf Bultmann emphasized the Christ of faith as being more important than the historical Jesus. In this case, the subjective encounter and *inner light* experience are more important than the so-called *dead letter* of the Bible.[14] One historical example is the early Quaker or Friends movement of the seventeenth century. Their desire for the immediacy of God's Spirit experienced through quietism was pursued at the expense of any clear doctrinal affirmation. This had the consequence of at least one expression of the Quaker movement becoming very liberal and universalistic.

THE AUTHORITY OF SCRIPTURE

It is clear that for most Christians, the matter of the authority of Scripture has been normative in the church. They agree that the Word of God is the only rule for life and faith, even if it is sometimes a problem as to how we hear and understand such an ancient document.[15]

---

13. Olson, *Mosaic*, 79.
14. Olson, *Mosaic*, 80.
15. Brueggemann, *Book that Breathes*, 37.

General and Special Revelation

There is some disagreement among Christians about whether divine revelation is complete or continuing. Did it stop in the past or is it continuing into the present? Karl Barth included the preaching of the church as part of the revelation of God. And what about the role of prophecy? Is the time of the prophets over, or are there still prophets operating in the church of Jesus Christ?

Ephesians 4:11–12: [11] "And he gave some, apostles; and some, prophets; and some, evangelists; and some, pastors and teachers; [12] For the perfecting of the saints, for the work of the ministry, for the edifying of the body of Christ." *KJV.*

Do prophecies in the church still count as part of divine revelation? Many Pentecostal and charismatic Christians believe that God does still communicate through prophetic utterances in the church. In the twentieth century, healing evangelists such as Oral Roberts encouraged openness to God, to speak out new revelation and prophetic words. Others have been fearful that encouraging this kind of new revelation could result in cultish practices beyond the bounds of Scriptural teaching.

There may be differing viewpoints on this question. Many Christians who accept the teaching about Jesus Christ and salvation in him, hold opposing understandings in this debate. Even the great theologians Barth and Brunner disagreed on the question of general revelation. So, it should not be surprising that we will come across Christians who hold different views from us in the question of revelation, while still holding to classical Christian doctrines.

What we can assume is that general revelation from God does exist, as Paul wrote in Romans 1. However, our source for Christian belief is God's special revelation in Jesus Christ and Scripture, and the preaching of the church finds its true source in these. Many of the questions that we ask in theology, and that we discussed earlier, such as 'what is our purpose in life?' may arise out of universal revelation. People are asking questions such as, 'Is there a God who cares and has revealed himself to those he has created?'

The preaching of the church draws out answers to these questions, even if we sometimes see from different points of view. As long as the revelation in Jesus Christ is kept central in our Christian discipleship, God will surely continue to speak to us and guide us into all truth by the indwelling Holy Spirit, who has been given to us.

God is at work to transform us to become more like his Son Jesus Christ. We will need to be open to this growth and transformation, which will mean we learn daily to know and understand God's Word and be made new creatures in him, by means of this process of renewal.

WOLFHART PANNENBERG

Wolfhart Pannenberg, (1928–2014) was a German Lutheran theologian who made several significant contributions to modern theology, including his concept of history as a form of revelation, centered on the resurrection of Jesus Christ. He also supported the thinking of contemporary anthropology with the concept of *openness to the world* which referred to the human ability to experience the environment in new ways. This is linked to our self-transcendence, which makes us distinct from animals.

As human beings, we are never satisfied with the present and are always seeking the new and the not-yet, which surpasses the present.[16] The question has been asked whether this *openness to the world* can be seen as a mark of the reality of God in the life of every human being. Has God created the world and human beings in such a way that his stamp is on them? Is it possible that to some limited extent human beings can know the creator God through their human experience?

Contemporary theologians are reasserting the idea that our existence presupposes that we are directed beyond this world for our ultimate fulfillment. They are echoing something that has already been said throughout Christian tradition by people such as Augustine, who declared that our hearts are restless until they find their rest in God. This great church father knew that there is a *God-shaped vacuum* in the heart of every person.

STUDY QUESTIONS

1. What do you understand by general revelation?
2. Why is special revelation of great importance?
3. What are the dangers of embracing new revelations that replace special revelation?
4. How do you understand the concept of spiritual transformation?

---

16. Grenz, *Theology*, 131–132.

PART TWO
Theology in History

Chapter 5

Historical Overview

WE WILL BE UNFOLDING the idea of Christian theology as a historical exploration including the emergence of the Christian church and different branches of theology.

THEOLOGY THROUGH HISTORY

The study of Christian Theology is sometimes seen as a historical survey, rooted in all the Scriptures and homing in on the birth of Jesus, his life, death, resurrection, ascension into heaven, and his coming again to this earth. It continues with the establishment of the church and its missionary outreach, as found in the missionary journeys and writings of the apostles and the book of Acts. We move onto church history and begin with the Patristic period, named after the fathers of the early church.

As Christians, we are shaped by the Christian story, which is an overarching story of the reality of God's dealing with his people, from creation right through to redemption. Theology consists of the reflections of many people from that Biblical narrative right up to contemporary Christianity, to try and answer what God has been up to and what his promised future is for his church and his world.[1]

As we get to know the stories of the people who have followed Jesus Christ through different cultures and in the history of the past two thousand years, we begin to grasp that this is a rich and at times turbulent journey of faith seeking understanding. One way of pursuing this journey is to

---

1. Olson, *Story of Christian Theology*, 11.

Part Two: Theology in History

follow the story of Christian beliefs to recover a sense of what it means to belong in the story of God's journey with his people.

THE PARTING OF THE WAYS

While Christianity was regarded as a branch of Judaism it was legally protected. As the hostility of the Jewish hierarchy towards those who believed in Jesus grew, there was a parting of the ways between the two groups. Patzia shows that there was great diversity in early Christianity, and the churches of the first century varied in their theology and praxis.[2]

As we read through the book of Acts it is evident that the relationship between Jewish Christianity and Judaism began to change after the outpouring of the Holy Spirit at Pentecost. While many Jews responded to Peter's sermon to repent and be baptized in the name of the Lord Jesus, not all were convinced that Jesus was the Jewish Messiah. Those who did not believe Peter's message questioned Peter and John's right to preach and to heal. The Jewish leaders imprisoned and flogged them.[3] Their animosity grew, and severe persecution arose against the church in Jerusalem and further afield, with Saul driving on this agenda.

Stephen, a Hellenistic Jewish believer in Jesus, gave a speech on the significance of the death of Jesus, and he added a critique of the temple.[4] This led to his martyrdom and the persecution of like-minded Hellenistic believers.[5]

In 62 CE, James, the brother of Jesus and the leader of the Christian community in Jerusalem was executed for refusing to deny that Jesus was the Messiah.[6] His death was a blow to the community of Jesus' followers, particularly as James was Jewish, and showed that a commitment to Jesus did not mean you had to sever your Jewish roots. He wrote the Letter of James in the New Testament. This letter shows the importance of an ethical faith that is rooted in faith in Jesus Christ and needs to be worked out in very practical ways while asking God for wisdom.

James 1:2–5: "My brothers and sisters, whenever you face trials of any kind, consider it nothing but joy, because you know that the testing of your

2. Patzia, *Emergence of the Church*, 144.
3. Acts 4:18–31
4. Acts 6:8–8:4
5. Patzia, *Emergence of the Church*, 148.
6. Davidson, *Birth of the Church*, 131.

faith produces endurance; and let endurance have its full effect, so that you may be mature and complete, lacking in nothing. If any of you is lacking in wisdom, ask God, who gives to all generously and ungrudgingly, and it will be given you." *NRSV.*

Just two years later, the emperor Nero blamed the Christians for the huge and devastating fire in Rome in 64 CE, resulting in persecution and martyrdom for many in Rome. From this time the Emperors of Rome viewed Christianity as criminal, and Christians were liable to punishment if they did not agree to sacrifice to the Emperor. Some Emperors were more tolerant of the Christian church than others.

The split between the two faiths became unavoidable, with the declaration of the followers of Jesus that he is the Messiah, Savior, and Son of God. There was no place within post Second Temple Judaism to either accept or tolerate this degree of diversity. With the destruction of the second temple in 70 CE, both Judaism and the new faith in Jesus as the Messiah that had emerged from within it were faced with an existential crisis. When the Jewish council convened at Jamnia (Yavneh) in c. 90 CE to discuss the way forward, the canon of the Hebrew Bible was finalized, and it was also decided to exclude believers in Jesus as Messiah from synagogue attendance. Consequently, the parting of the ways became inevitable.

THE PATRISTIC PERIOD OF THEOLOGY

The Patristic period of theology was c.100–450 CE. The abbreviation CE stands for the Common Era. This is the time after the birth of Christ and is sometimes known as AD, which is an abbreviation for *Anno Domini,* a Latin phrase meaning 'in the year of our Lord,' referring to the year of Christ's birth. Thus, we can see how important the coming of Jesus Christ has been in our calendar.

Early Christians thought about the Jewish Scriptures, the events of the life of Jesus, and the establishment of the Christian church. They were known as the fathers of the church who were the first theologians. Latin for fathers is *patres,* and this is why this time was called the *Patristic* period. Because they lived so close to the time of the early church they are often referred to by later thinkers. They thought deeply about issues such as the authority, the nature, and extent of the canon of Scripture and of tradition. The canon of Scripture was the set of books to be included in Scripture, and it included a long process for both Jews and Christians, with much discussion and some disputes too.

This period in church history was important because it laid early foundations for the rest of Christian theology. It dealt with some fascinating characters such as Justin Martyr (c.100–c.165) and Irenaeus of Lyons (c.120–c.202), among others. By the way, if you are puzzled about the c., that stands for *circa*, meaning 'about,' because sometimes we are not quite sure of the exact date of births and deaths when the people concerned lived so long ago.

JUSTIN MARTYR

Justin Martyr was an important second century apologist. The apologists were philosophers and thinkers who addressed their contemporary culture with a defense of the Christian faith. They tried to create a bridge between Christianity and Greek philosophy and Judaism.[7]

Justin was called the martyr due to his witness to Christ, which led to his martyrdom in Rome in 165 CE. He was born in Samaria and lived for a time in Ephesus. One of his books was his *Dialogue with Trypho*, presenting his arguments for Christianity against the objections of the Jewish faith. It was written in the form of a conversation with Trypho, an educated Hellenistic Jew, around 135 CE.

Justin was a student of philosophy. While studying Platonism he read about the Hebrew prophets. He became fascinated by them, as they were more ancient than the philosophers and gave an explanation of the beginning and end of all things and those matters which the philosophers ought to know. He believed that whatever philosophers had to say about the ultimate questions of life they received from the writings of the prophets. He argued that the transcendent and mysterious God, spoken of by the Platonist philosophers, is the God of biblical revelation.

Justin challenged the idea that the Christian faith was merely superstition and inferior to the best philosophies. Contrary to that thinking, "the right principles that philosophers and lawgivers have discovered and expressed they owe to whatever of the Word they have found and contemplated in part. The reason they have contradicted each other is that they have not known the entire Word, which is Christ."[8]

---

7. Kärkkäinen, *Doctrine of God*, 65–66.

8. Martyr, *Writings of Justin Martyr*, loc. 1077.

This Word he called the *Logos* was present in the patriarchs, prophets, and philosophers and became incarnate in Jesus Christ. Justin realized that the prophets were filled with the Holy Spirit, and they glorified God, the Father of all things and the creator, and his Son the Christ.[9] In his account of turning to the Christian faith, Justin shows how the ancient prophetic writings gave him a love for the prophets, who in turn pointed him to Christ. He was convinced that Christianity was the oldest and truest of the philosophies. His *Apology* was addressed to Emperor Pius c.151, to defend Christianity from the Roman government's antagonism and any pagan criticisms.

Justin came from a heathen background before he came to faith in Jesus Christ. He maintained the truth of Christianity from the fulfillment of Old Testament prophecy. He also argued against the idea that Christians were cannibals and that they practiced incest. He showed that they were moral and obedient to God, they cared for one another and prayed for their enemies. Their worship did not use magic or immoral practices.

Justin described the Eucharist or thanksgiving, which was taken in bread and wine to remember the death of Jesus Christ, and the fact that they had prayers and readings from the apostles and the prophets. They also took a collection for those in need. His writings provide a useful picture of the Eucharist or Lord's Supper service on a Sunday and how it was led.[10]

> And this food is called among us *Eucharistia* [the Eucharist], of which no one is allowed to partake but the man who believes that the things which we teach are true, and who has been washed with the washing that is for the remission of sins, and unto regeneration, and who is living as Christ has enjoined.[11]

BRANCHES OF THEOLOGY

Apart from interesting characters during this period, there were also some fierce debates about the authority of the church, the Bible, and church tradition. They were looking at questions such as, 'What does it mean to be the church?' and 'What about the sacraments, such as Christian baptism and

---

9. Walker, *History of the Christian Church*, 46.
10. Davidson, *Birth of the Church*, 214.
11. Martyr, *Writings of Justin Martyr*, loc. 872-882.

the Lord's Supper?' They also discussed what it means to be a human being and how we gain salvation. These discussions later led to branches of theology such as the study of the church (Ecclesiology), the study of salvation (Soteriology), the study of the work of the Holy Spirit (Pneumatology), the study of humankind and the created world (Anthropology), and the study of the consummation of creation (Eschatology).

THE WORK OF THE HOLY SPIRIT

The work of the Holy Spirit is of great importance, for without his empowering there would be no spread of the gospel and no faith in Jesus in the world. When Jesus was preparing to leave the world he spoke to his disciples and entrusted to them the task of making disciples of all nations. His final words, before ascending from the Mount of Olives into heaven, were that they were to be his witnesses to the ends of the earth.[12] They would not be alone in this mission, for the Holy Spirit would be sent to them as a counselor, to teach them, and to remind them of all the things that Jesus had taught them. He would guide them into all truth. He would not speak on his own, but he would make known to them all that Jesus had to say to them, just as Jesus had communicated to them all that the Father had told him. Just as the prophets of old were able to say, "Thus says the LORD", so the disciples would know with assurance what Jesus wanted them to say.

On the day of Pentecost, the Holy Spirit was poured out on the disciples, so that they could go out and share the good news of Jesus Christ with people from many different nations and in many different languages.

In 1 Corinthians 2:9–13, Paul was able to write about things that God had revealed to the disciples by his Holy Spirit. These things were not what entered into the perception of human beings through what they heard or saw naturally, but rather the deep things of God. This was communicated to them to show them what things were freely given to them by God. As a result of what the Spirit spoke into their innermost hearts, they gained spiritual insight that would never have been taught by the world.

The Holy Spirit revealed the things of God and inspired the apostles so that they were able to teach and preach and also write the gospels and letters that make up the New Testament.

We can never prove to others that Jesus is God's Son. That is the work of the Holy Spirit who opens the spiritually blind eyes of men and women

12. Acts 1:8

to convince them of the truth of the gospel. When the gospel is preached, the Holy Spirit is at work in the hearts and minds of those who listen. He also guides us as we read the Word of God and is our teacher.

The Holy Spirit convicts the world about sin and of righteousness and judgment.[13] Thus he works in our lives to convict us when we do wrong or have wrong attitudes and helps us to turn from sin and walk in the ways of God.

The early church was proclaiming Jesus as Lord but was also thinking about questions such as how he could be divine and human at the same time. This also led to discussions about the nature of God and the doctrine of the Trinity. Out of these deep discussions came the formulation of doctrines such as the doctrine of atonement, or what it means to say that Jesus died for us, and the doctrine of God, in trying to explain and understand how God can be one and three at the same time.

INTERPRETING THE CHRISTIAN FAITH

Part of our mission as theologians is to interpret the Christian faith and tradition to the world. In every culture of the world, there is a need for Christianity to be presented. To do this, we need to understand the gospel and be able to communicate it fully even when our faith is challenged.

> By refreshing our vision of God, theology ensures that we constantly present faith as a dynamic, transformative reality to our culture. We speak of God, not in terms of the wooden repetition of the past, but with the excitement and passion of discovery and commitment.[14]

The development of a good theological understanding is of the utmost importance. The place that Scripture holds has become critical. We are exhorted by the Apostle Paul in 2 Timothy 2:15, "Study to shew thyself approved unto God, a workman that needeth not to be ashamed, rightly dividing the word of truth." *KJV.*

Abraham Heschel encourages both Jews and Christians to develop a renewed love for the Hebrew Bible, and as Christian believers, we need to add that the New Testament needs to be placed together with the Hebrew Scriptures.

---

13. John 16:8
14. McGrath, *Mere Theology,* 23.

Heschel's hope is that Judaism and Christianity will develop in the future towards a profound expression of mutual esteem without denying their disparity and that this will become a means of helping each other in their understanding of their discrete differences and commitments and growth in their cherishing of what God means.[15]

We realize that the struggle that we are facing is something that affects all people of faith who desire not only to know God but also to cherish what he means to us.

STUDY QUESTIONS

1. When was the Patristic period of theology?
2. Explain the parting of the ways between Judaism and Christianity and what the consequences were for the church?
3. Discuss the ideas of Justin Martyr and their importance for Christianity?
4. Discuss the development of the understanding of the work of the Holy Spirit.

---

15. Mechanic, *Quest*, 169.

Chapter 6

The Spread of Gnosticism

THE SECOND CENTURY PRODUCED great Christian leaders such as Polycarp and Irenaeus. We deal in-depth with Irenaeus's response to Gnosticism and issues of redemption and salvation, to help us understand how Gnosticism became a distortion of the teaching of the church.

POLYCARP

In the second century CE, Polycarp was an important link to one of the disciples of the Lord, John, who was the last of the apostles to die.[1] Polycarp had been taught by John and he was therefore like a living link to Jesus and his apostles. There was at that time no Christian Bible as such, other than letters which were circulated, the gospel accounts, and the Hebrew Scriptures, that later became known to Christians as the Old Testament.

Polycarp was able to share information with others about what the apostles taught and how they established the early churches. He, in turn, trained up new leaders in the Christian faith. This teaching was known as the oral tradition and was important in determining the teachings of the early church.

IRENAEUS

Irenaeus was born in about 120 CE in Asia Minor and learned the teachings of the apostle John from bishop Polycarp. Irenaeus was sent far from

---

1. Olson, *Story of Christian Theology*, 68–69.

his hometown to Lyon, in southern Gaul, to become an elder among other Christian emigrants from Smyrna, who had come to live in the Rhone valley. He became a leader among the Christians and bishop of Lyon in about 177 CE.

Irenaeus was sent to Rome to protest against heresies that were coming into the church in the Rhone valley and it was this that saved his life. Thousands of Christians in the Rhone valley lost their lives in 177 CE, in a persecution by Emperor Marcus Aurelius.

While in Rome, Irenaeus met up with a man who was previously a disciple of Polycarp. This man left Christianity as taught by the apostles, to join a Gnostic cult under Valentinus. When Irenaeus returned to Gaul, he was appalled to find that this Gnostic cult was affecting the faith and thinking of Christians there too.

Irenaeus wrote two major writings that survive. *Refutation and Overthrow of Knowledge Falsely So-called* is generally known as *Against Heresies* and is a series of five books exposing and overthrowing Gnosticism and remaining faithful to the apostolic witness in the face of the opposition presented by non-Christian interpretations. *Proof of the Apostolic Preaching* is an instructional book showing that the Christian faith fulfills the Old Testament.[2]

The word Gnostic is a modern term to cover several second century sects that had common elements. This movement had its roots in the first century. The major issues that became the subject of the debate were the Gnostic teachings that there were two Gods and two Christs, the nature of redemption, and the essence of evil. The Gnostics were world-rejecting and transcendentalist in outlook.[3]

The Gnostics thought they possessed a higher spiritual knowledge than that of the other church leaders of their time. They believed that Christ only appeared to be human, but that he was not God incarnate as Jesus. This belief resulted in a division in the Christian church.

The syncretism of Hellenistic (Greek) religions began entering Christianity when the gospel was taken to the Gentiles and much of the Gnostic teaching was partly Christianised. Not all Gnosticism was Christian, and it also existed independently from the church. From the point of view of the

---

2. Walker, *History*, 16.
3. Walker et al., *History*, 61.

second century Christian writers it may, however, have looked like a heresy within the church.[4]

GNOSTIC TEACHING

Irenaeus is one of the Christian writers who is an important source of our knowledge of Gnosticism. The Gnostic teaching delighted in the obscure, complex, and mystifying, and not everyone was said to be capable of the 'knowledge.' It took the form of a story about the transcendent, which used abstract philosophical or theological ideas, that were given names and woven into the tale.

The creation story figures in Gnostic thinking, but there are two different worlds having two different deities. The God-figure of the material world was also called the Demi-urge and could be equated with the God of the Jewish Scriptures. He claimed to be the one true God. The Gnostics argued he was made of soul material and was ignorant of the Mind which made the spirit-world and its inhabitants.

In his *Demonstration of the Apostolic Preaching*, Irenaeus argued that salvation from the time of creation to the end of history was the work of the one true God, who was the creator and redeemer.

In his book *Against the Heresies*, Irenaeus wrote that the Christian God was the same God as Yhwh, often translated as LORD, the God of the Jews and that he revealed himself through Jesus, which accords with Scriptural teaching.

Irenaeus taught the rule of faith and from the Scriptures, that God the creator contains all things while being himself limited by nothing. The creator God, who is not distant but rather intimately present, called the world into being, out of nothing, and the world is not some distant spiritual Fulness, as the Gnostics called it, but this visible cosmos. In his book *Demonstration of the Apostolic Preaching*, Irenaeus speaks of the distinct yet related roles of the Father, Son, and Holy Spirit.

> *God the Father uncreated*, who is uncontained, invisible, one God, creator of the universe, this is the first article of our faith . . . and the *Word of God*, the Son of God, our Lord Jesus Christ . . . in the fullness of time, to gather all things to himself, he became a human being amongst human beings, capable of being seen and touched, to destroy death, bring life, and restore fellowship between God

4. Walker et al., *History*, 63–64.

and humanity. And . . . the *Holy Spirit* . . . who, in the fullness of time, was poured out in a new way on our human nature in order to renew humanity throughout the entire world in the sight of God.[5]

ISSUES OF REDEMPTION AND SALVATION

The issues of redemption and salvation became disputed. This was of importance to people who lived in a world that appeared to be governed by chance and demons, and who wanted to know that they were saved. The Gnostics claimed to be able to tell them the answer that they sought. They divided the resurrection into spiritual and physical or fleshly. They saw it as an incomplete system in which the Jews and Greeks put their trust. The followers of the Gnostic leader Valentinus claimed the following:

> [I]t is not only baptism that frees (from the power of fate) but Gnosis — knowledge of what we were, why we came into being, where we are, and at what point we have been placed (in the cosmos), whither we are hastening, from what we have been redeemed, and what is birth and rebirth.[6]

They believed that they were displaced spirit-selves who had lost their way from the world of light and knowledge and now found themselves in the cosmos of darkness and ignorance and needed to find their way to their true home. They taught that the redemption that Christians understand, is a shadow of the redemptive drama unfolding in the hidden spirit-world. To return to this spirit-world would require revelation leading to self-awareness and ultimately restoration. This pathway would only be open to the elect who are set apart and are superior even to the creator God of the Jewish Scriptures.

> They classified humans into three classes — first, pagans who were headed for destruction, second, ordinary Christian believers who were considered second class and belonged to the God of the Jewish Scriptures and lived at the soul level along with God, and third, the Gnostics who were the 'spirituals' and were headed for the Fulness of the divine world.[7]

5. McGrath, *Christian Theology Reader*, 296.
6. Frend, *Early Church*, 50.
7. Walker et al., *History*, 64–65.

The Spread of Gnosticism

Basilides and Valentinus believed that it was a fall or error in the higher spiritual realm that had produced the cosmos or darkness in the world. They explained this process using a myth, in which the lowest member of the light world, called Sophia or wisdom, desired to know the unknowable Father. To be redeemed, this error had to be exiled to the inferior and lower cosmos called the Void. Here the spiritual elements were trapped in the soul and matter. The Void was an imitation or shadow of the real spirit world or Fulness, and it was in the visible cosmos.

They also believed there were two Christs. One was a psychic Christ who was the Messiah promised by the God of the Jewish faith, and the other was the true Savior, who descended on him from the Fulness at his baptism.

IRENAEUS RESPONDS TO THE GNOSTICS

In response to this teaching, Irenaeus wrote extensively on the ransom theory of the atonement. He taught how Christ himself is alone able to teach us divine things and to redeem us:

> For in no other way could we have learned the things of God, unless our Master, existing as the Word, had become man. For no other being had the power of revealing to us the things of the Father, except His own proper Word. For what other person "knew the mind of the Lord," or who else "has become His counsellor?"[8]

Irenaeus believed that the prophetic and apostolic Scriptures would refute heretical teachings if the Scripture was interpreted in the plain sense and the obscure passages understood in their obvious meaning.

Like many of the other church leaders of his day, Irenaeus saw Christian Gnosticism as a distortion of the church's teaching-tradition. The church leaders opposed the dualistic notion of two Gods and two Christs, and they did not like to be considered second-class psychics. Another problem was the criticism of the Jewish Scriptures by the Gnostics. This was an attack on God's self-revelation in history.

---

8. Irenaeus, *Against Heresies,* loc. 8118.

Part Two: Theology in History

IRENAEUS'S THEORY OF REDEMPTION

Irenaeus explored the idea of recapitulation in Christ. This meant for him something like going over again. Where Adam failed in his obedience to God, as we read in Genesis 3, Christ recapitulates the history of Adam in becoming a human being, but he was completely obedient to his heavenly Father. He succeeded at every point, including overcoming every temptation. Ultimately his obedience to the Father's will meant that he died on the cross to take away the sins of all of humanity. Where the salvation of humanity was lost in Adam's disobedience to God, it was regained in Christ.

> But when he [Christ] was incarnate and became a human being, he recapitulated in himself . . . the long history of the human race, obtaining salvation for us so that we might regain in Jesus Christ what we had lost in Adam, that is, being in the image and likeness of God.[9]

While the Gnostics did not hold out much hope for the human race as a whole but only for a few elite spirits who had the special knowledge, Irenaeus in his anti-Gnostic theory of redemption showed that redemption in Christ was to transform and save all of humanity. Irenaeus believed and taught that what Adam did in the Garden of Eden (Genesis 3) and what Jesus Christ did in his life and his death, affected all other human beings because the first Adam and Jesus Christ, the second Adam, were fountainheads of humanity.[10]

The background of this theory of redemption can be found in Paul's letter to the Romans in chapter 5, where he reflects on Adam and Christ. Irenaeus's theory of recapitulation is an interpretation of Romans 5.

Romans 5:15–16: [15]"But the gift is not like the trespass. For if the many died by the trespass of the one man, how much more did God's grace and the gift that came by the grace of the one man, Jesus Christ, overflow to the many! [16] Nor can the gift of God be compared with the result of one man's sin: The judgment followed one sin and brought condemnation, but the gift followed many trespasses and brought justification." *NIV.*

---

9. McGrath, *Christian Theology Reader*, 177.
10. Olson, *Story of Christian Theology*, 75–76.

THE SPREAD OF GNOSTICISM

CHRIST THE SECOND ADAM

Christ is the second Adam of the human race. Irenaeus shows that he recapitulates in himself his ancient formation of humankind (Adam) to kill sin and deprive death of its power and overcome the corruption of Adam's life. He did this by living the reverse of Adam's corruption through life-giving obedience. In this way, the fall was reversed and humanity, that fell because of Adam, could now be renewed. Irenaeus taught that for humankind to be saved it was necessary for God, who has life, to enter into Adam the man, who is like us in every way. He hungers and thirsts, eats and drinks, is wearied and needs rest, knows anxiety, sorrow and joy, and suffers pain when confronted with death. Without his incarnation, Christ could not have reversed the fall of Adam. Christ went through the whole scope of human life from conception to birth, childhood, adulthood, and death. At every stage, he reversed the disobedience of Adam. Irenaeus saw the event of Satan's temptation of Jesus in the wilderness as pivotal. Satan had tempted Adam and Eve in the garden, and they capitulated to his deceit and fell into disobedience to God. By contrast, when Satan came to Jesus to tempt him, Jesus remained obedient to the will of his Father. This passage from Luke 4 is the last of the recorded temptations directed to Jesus while in the wilderness.

Luke 4:9–13: [9] "And he brought him to Jerusalem, and set him on a pinnacle of the temple, and said unto him, If thou be the Son of God, cast thyself down from hence: [10]For it is written, He shall give his angels charge over thee, to keep thee: [11]And in their hands they shall bear thee up, lest at any time thou dash thy foot against a stone. [12]And Jesus answering said unto him, It is said, Thou shalt not tempt the Lord thy God. [13]And when the devil had ended all the temptation, he departed from him for a season." KJV.

IRENAEUS'S VISION OF SALVATION

McGrath helps us to consider the concept of the economy of salvation. This "sets out the idea that God's interaction with the world is described in terms of a narrative of creation, fall, redemption and final consummation."[11] He shows that Irenaeus picked up on what is fully developed in the New Testament and explained it in reaction to the Gnostic interpretations of salvation

---

11. McGrath: *Surprised by Meaning*, 54.

history. "Irenaeus laid out a panoramic vision of the economy of salvation, insisting that the entire breadth of history, from creation to consummation, was the work of one and the same triune God."[12]

Jesus remained obedient right to the point of his death and resurrection, which were the culmination of his victory over sin and death. This opens the door for those who choose to follow Christ through repentance and faith, to receive that transformation that the Son of God made possible. They enter into a new humanity with the hope of sharing in God's divine nature through the gift of salvation through Jesus Christ.

Later in this book, we shall look further at who Jesus is and what the work was that his Father in heaven sent him to this earth to achieve. Our faith needs to grow not only in head knowledge but also in our heart's response. Mind and heart need to be involved in faith, and we thus study theology with personal knowledge of God in faith, leading to the worship of God.

STUDY QUESTIONS

1. Why was Polycarp important in theology?
2. What were Irenaeus's greatest contributions to the Christian church?
3. Explain Irenaeus's theory of redemption?
4. Why did Irenaeus see Satan's temptation of Jesus in the wilderness as pivotal in his explanation of redemption?

---

12. McGrath: *Surprised by Meaning*, 54.

Chapter 7

North African Thinkers

IN THIS CHAPTER, WE look at Christianity in North Africa in the third century and the forces that impeded and prospered the spread of Christianity in that area. We discuss the controversy between Clement of Alexandria and Tertullian and the importance of the work of Origen.

CHRISTIANITY IN NORTH AFRICA

By the beginning of the third century, Christianity was thriving in North Africa. By 185 CE a Christian catechetical school arose in Alexandria, under the leadership of a converted Stoic philosopher named Pantaenus. Philosophy and religion were influencing each other. Two Christian teachers living in Alexandria were Clement and Origen. They tried to show that the best of Greek thought was compatible with Christianity, although Christianity was superior to other world views.

Across the Mediterranean Sea from Rome was the North African city of Carthage. Here the philosophy of Stoicism was of wide interest. Justice and morality were upheld. Christians in Carthage were influenced by this as they worked towards a moral and community-minded lifestyle. Leading Christian thinkers in the area of Carthage were Tertullian and Cyprian. Their writings influenced people in Rome and further afield in the Latin speaking part of the Roman empire.

Although the influence of these thinkers took Christianity forward, persecution on a large scale under the Roman Emperors Decius and Diocletian meant that Christianity was forced underground, and its progress impeded. Various heresies also threatened the Christian faith.

Yet despite severe persecution and some martyrdoms, such as that of the great Christian leader Cyprian, the church was not stamped out as the Roman leaders had hoped. Buildings known as basilicas were constructed for worship. At this time, decisions were being made about what books were to be included in Scripture, and bishops that were given larger areas to look after were now called archbishops. By the end of the third century, Christianity had spread to nearly every region of the Roman empire.

MONTANISM

In Carthage, Montanism flourished. Even Christian leaders such as Tertullian were said to be influenced by it, although there is no proof of that. Montanus, the leader of this movement, claimed that the Holy Spirit spoke directly through him and that his prophecies were as inspired as the words of the Hebrew prophets and the New Testament writers of Scripture. This was called the "New Prophecy" movement in the second century, and it continued to pose a strong threat to church leaders. Montanism is not the only movement in Church history where people have claimed that their prophecies are equal to Scripture.[1] The Morman Church of Jesus Christ of Latter-Day Saints is a modern Montanist type of movement, as they claim to be Christian but consider the writings of their founder, Joseph Smith, and other prophets in their church to be equal in authority to the Bible.

In the 1970s the Jesus People Movement that arose in America had Gnostic-like teachings and Montanist-like prophets that brought prophetic messages. They considered themselves to be a new form of Christianity, with the authority to decide what people should believe and how they should live their lives. This group was not considered to be an authentic expression of Christianity by most Protestant churches in America.

PHILOSOPHY AND CHRISTIAN THEOLOGY

Despite this erratic forward movement in the life of the church, there was a point of controversy between two of the great Christian thinkers, Clement of Alexandria and Tertullian of Carthage. This was the relationship between philosophy and Christian theology. Clement was influenced by the second century apologist and martyr Justin, who saw Christianity as the

---

1. Olson, *Mosaic*, 59.

true philosophy that fulfills the best of Greek philosophy. He understood the philosophies of Socrates and Plato as a preparation for the gospel and as useful for Christian thinkers.

Tertullian took an opposite view towards pagan philosophy and he famously said, "What, indeed, has Athens to do with Jerusalem?" He saw the dangers in trying to accommodate Greek philosophy with the Christian faith, as some of the second century apologists had done. The Jewish scholar Philo who lived at the time of Jesus Christ, in Alexandria, had tried to join Judaism and Greek philosophy. His influence may have affected the Alexandrian Christians in the second and third centuries as they tried to explain the Bible and their faith philosophically.

CLEMENT OF ALEXANDRIA

Clement of Alexandria, who had been a pupil of Pantaenus, became head of the Christian catechetical school around 200, but he fled Alexandria in 202 to avoid persecution. He wrote five books for the students at the Christian school in Alexandria. *Exhortation to the Heathen* is against heathenism, superstitions, and idolatrous beliefs. In his books, he presents a positive slant on Greek philosophy, showing that what Socrates and Plato spoke truly had been borrowed from Moses or directly inspired by God and his Word.

The book *The Instructor* discusses Jesus as the Word of God and the wisdom of God, whose main role in salvation was to exhort humans to live a spiritual life of obedience and reasonable actions, as taught by the Word. This book provides us with information on how Christians were expected to behave and on the customs of the age.[2] One of the reasons why Clement included Platonism in his interpretation of the Christian faith is that it rejected the immoral gods and goddesses of the Greeks and Romans.

There were a few areas in which Clement was controversial in his theology. He called the Christian 'the true or perfect Gnostic.' While some people have accused him of being an ally of the second century Gnostics, this is unlikely. He was using the term to describe the person who lives a life of wisdom and who shuns the lower life of bodily desires and material gain. He showed that the goal of salvation is to share in the divine nature and gain immortality.

To attain this was a work of God, attained through the person yielding to God through contemplation and study. The teacher in this process is

2. Walker, *History*, 73.

Jesus Christ himself, the Word of the Father. Clement took a more Platonic view of humanity and creation than a biblical view, in that he emphasized the spiritual side to the detriment of the physical.

In his view of God, his Greek orientation is also seen. For him, God is passionless (free of desires and emotions) and he taught that we should also become so, through self-control. This view of God does not match up with the description of God in Scripture. There he is seen as loving, vengeful, and showing many other emotions. Jesus is also shown as angry in the temple when he overthrew the tables of the money changers. He was moved with compassion and cried out on the cross.

ORIGEN

Origen was born c. 185 and grew up with a knowledge of the Bible and studied philosophy from an early age. Much of what we know of his background comes to us through Eusebius, who devoted most of the sixth book of *Ecclesiastical History* to him. Origen was about seventeen when a bloody persecution of the Church in Alexandria broke out. His father was put in prison and finally martyred, leaving Origen to work to support his mother and younger brothers. He became a teacher at a young age. He gave private teaching and as a catechist helped prepare those wishing to become Christians.[3] He lived an extremely ascetic life.

In 215 CE, Origen went to Caesarea but was allowed to return to Alexandria where he continued to teach. He lived during a turbulent time in Church history when Christians were suffering persecution. In 230 he was banished from Alexandria and found a home in Caesarea in 232, where he studied, taught, and preached frequently. He worked on his composition of the *Commentaries* including his *Commentary on St John* and later his *Commentary on St Matthew*. He produced the monumental work the *Hexapla*, which gave the Hebrew and four parallel translations of the Old Testament and a long series of commentaries and notes, covering nearly the whole of Scripture. The homilies were on the texts of Scripture, and Origen was said to preach very regularly. He has been called the father of the homily. Some of his writings have perished, and we now have only two of his letters. There is an entire treatise *On prayer*, and an *Exhortation to Martyrdom* sent to his friend Ambrose who was a prisoner for his faith.

---

3. McGuckin, *Handbook to Origen*, 4.

Contra Celsum [*Against Celsus*] was Origen's convincing defense of the Christian faith against the criticism of the Platonist Celsus. Celsus had desired to discredit Christianity and spoke of secret associations that Christians entered into with each other, that were contrary to law. He also attempted to bring into disrepute the love-feasts of the Christians.[4]

Origen used philosophic principles that he brought into harmony with the Scriptures. He used allegorical interpretations of the Scriptures, through which he attempted to delve deeply into the meaning. In the fundamentals of the faith, he did not differ from the church and apostolic traditions. On these essential Christian beliefs, he built his systematic theology. He emphasized the sacrifice of the death of Jesus but interpreted it in several different ways. Some Christian leaders in his day criticized his ideas. His theological structure is today seen as a great intellectual achievement.

"Origen . . . is widely regarded as one of the early church's most influential and creative interpreters of Scripture. Origen here uses the imagery of "body, mind and spirit" to distinguish three different ways in which Scripture may be read, according to the maturity of the reader in question."[5]

Great teachers, such as St Gregory of Nazianzus and St Jerome, gave expression to Origen's opinions. While many admired his scholarship and praised him, there were others, such as St Methodius, who wrote works against Origen, but his main adversaries were the heretics.

TERTULLIAN

Tertullian was born c. 150 CE and lived in Carthage. He was a lawyer and after his conversion to Christianity in about 190, he began to write a defense of the Christian faith. He took a very different approach to Clement. He showed the opposition between divine revelation and human thought, in contrast to Clement and Origen who looked for ways in which they could be brought together. Tertullian believed that very little truth could be found outside the biblical revelation that was inspired by God. He was afraid that if Christians studied philosophy they might be led into idolatry and even heresy.[6]

---

4. Origen, *Complete Works*, 385.
5. McGrath, *Christian Theology Reader*, 46.
6. Olson, *Story of Christian Theology*, 91–92.

PART TWO: THEOLOGY IN HISTORY

MARCION THE HERETIC

Another heretic, called Marcion, came to Rome about 139 CE, and his community soon spread. His teaching was much like that of the Gnostics and he became a rival to churches of orthodox persuasion. He tried to divide the God of the gospel and the God of Judaism, whom he saw as being harsh and inconsistent. He drew up his canon of sacred books for the New Testament which excluded the Pastoral Epistles (1 and 2 Timothy and Titus) but included a form of Luke's gospel. He rejected the deity described in the Hebrew Scriptures. His teaching forced the churches to consider the question of the continuation of the church from its Jewish heritage and the history of salvation, including both the Old and New Testaments.

AGAINST MARCION

Tertullian wrote an important work in five volumes called *Against Marcion*. Tertullian was very direct in his criticism of Marcion's views and writings. "Marcion has quenched the light of his faith, and so lost the God whom he had found."[7]

In contrast to Marcion's idea of two Gods, Tertullian proclaimed God to be one. He is "the great Supreme existing in eternity, unbegotten, unmade, without beginning, without end . . . God the great Supreme in form and in reason, and in might and in power."[8] Tertullian showed that Marcion's opinion was to pronounce God as some inferior being, to rob God of his attributes. The influence of Tertullian's writings has been immense throughout the Western Christian Church. He worked out the doctrine of the Trinity, which was largely forgotten about until the Eastern Christian Church came close to what Tertullian had said, but about one hundred years later.

THE HERESY OF PRAXEAS

Tertullian also wrote against the Roman teacher Praxeas, who tried to explain the doctrine of the Trinity and in the process reduced the Father, Son, and Holy Spirit to one person with three roles. This was known as

---

7. Tertullian, *Select Works*, loc. 7317.
8. Tertullian, *Select Works*, loc. 7348–7357.

modalism and was later taken up by a Christian in Rome called Sabellius and became known as Sabellianism.

Tertullian spoke of the Praxean heresy as being inspired by the devil who aims to destroy the truth. Praxeas maintained that there was only one Lord, the Almighty, creator of the world and he came down into the Virgin, was born of her, suffered, and was himself, Jesus Christ.

JESUS THE SON OF GOD

In the refutation of Praxeas, Tertullian argued that when the devil tempted Christ after John's baptism, he approached him as *the Son of God*, thus showing that God had a Son. Twice in Matthew 4, he calls him Son of God:

Matt. 4:3 "The tempter came and said to him, "If you are the Son of God, command these stones to become loaves of bread." "NRSV.

Matt. 4:6 "saying to him, "If you are the Son of God, throw yourself down; for it is written, 'He will command his angels concerning you,' and 'On their hands they will bear you up so that you will not dash your foot against a stone.'" NRSV.

Tertullian wrote of Praxeas's influence at Rome, where he "drove away prophecy, and he brought in heresy; he put to flight the Paraclete [Holy Spirit], and he crucified the Father."[9]

Tertullian explained that God is one and is heavenly. The *Logos* "is both God and God's offshoot through which he relates to creation."[10] He explained the relationship between the Father and the Son as being like the sun and a ray of sunshine that descended into the virgin. He was both God and human united. Tertullian's caution against human speculation was because he felt the revelation of God was very important to the Christian.

CONTROVERSY IN TERTULLIAN'S LIFE

One of the controversies in Tertullian's life, according to tradition, was that he left the Great Church of the bishops and joined the Montanist New Prophecy Church in Carthage. Yet his legacy lived on in other Christian thinkers who followed his ideas that human speculation could not be mixed with divine revelation.

---

9. Tertullian, *Select Works*, Loc. 17088.
10. Olson, *Story of Christian Theology*, 93.

Tertullian's theological attitude and mindset may be described as more close-minded toward the possibility of truth genuinely helpful to Christian life and thought found outside divine revelation . . . he did find little truth useful to Christianity outside of the biblical revelation God gave to Israel and the apostles, which he considered inspired and unique.[11]

Tertullian practiced a strict, ascetic discipline of life. The austerity that he advocated, like many of the African Fathers, led to a rigoristic approach to his faith. This mindset made it very difficult for him to reconcile what he saw as human philosophy with Scriptural truth that was of divine origin.

STUDY QUESTIONS

1. What forces both impeded and prospered the spread of Christianity in North Africa?

2. Discuss the points of controversy between Clement of Alexandria and Tertullian of Carthage.

3. What great contributions did Origen make to Christianity?

---

11. Olson, *Story of Christian Theology*, 91.

Chapter 8
The Controversy of Arianism

We chart the rise of Constantine, the first Christian Emperor who changed the course of history for the Christian church. The Arian controversy arose, and we see the important work of Athanasius and the council of Nicea.

DIOCLETIAN BECOMES ROMAN EMPEROR

In 284 CE, Diocletian became the Roman Emperor. He was a good administrator and set out to improve the army and the internal administration. With this in view, he appointed Maximian (Latin: *Maximianus*, c.250–c.310) as Augustus, and two more Caesars, one on the Rhine frontier and the other on the Danube frontier. He moved from Rome to Nicomedia in Asia Minor. He saw in the rapidly growing Church a political threat. There were two ways to control such a body of people. One would be to force it into submission and the other would be to create an alliance and thus secure political control of it, and this was what Diocletian decided on.

The eastern Caesar, Galerius, was very hostile to Christianity, and he may have been the one to persuade Diocletian to persecute the church and establish emperor worship. A period of persecution began in 303 CE. Churches were destroyed and sacred books confiscated. Clergy were captured and forced to offer sacrifice to the emperor or face torture. Once Diocletian retired and Maximian was forced to abdicate, persecution decreased in the west and increased in the east. Constantine was made emperor in 306 and went to war against Maxentius, the son of Maximian, in his struggle for the empire.

Part Two: Theology in History

BY THIS SIGN, YOU WILL CONQUER

Constantine had a kindly feeling towards Christians, and he desired the help of the Christian God in his struggle against Maxentius. In a dream, the night before the battle, he saw the initial letters of Christ's name and the words 'By this sign, you will conquer.' He painted this sign on the helmets and shields of the soldiers and won the battle. He saw the victory as the intervention of the Christian God.[1]

The Edict of Milan in 313 CE, provided freedom of conscience and placed Christianity on an equal footing with any religion in the Roman world. It also restored all confiscated church property. By 323 CE, Constantine was the sole ruler of the Roman world.

The church grew rapidly with the favor that Constantine showed it. By 321 CE, Sunday work was forbidden to those living in the cities. Gifts were given to the clergy and great churches began to be built. These favors were for the so-called 'Catholic church' and not for the various sects that had sprung up. Byzantium (today's Istanbul in Turkey) became Constantine's new capital, and it was a strongly Christian city. The bishop of Rome was left in Rome and became highly regarded by the Latin-speaking west.

THE INFLUENCE OF THE DONATISTS

In North Africa, the church was divided over leaders whom some considered had committed a mortal sin, by handing over copies of the Scriptures during the persecutions that had taken place previously. Those who argued that Christian leaders must be faultless for their ministry to be effective and for them to be able to minister in the church in prayer and in leading the services were known as the Donatists.

A large council met in southern Gaul in 314 CE, and the ordination of those who had been considered unworthy was now accepted. The persecution of Christians had died down, but the split between the Donatists and mainstream Christians had opened wide.

Augustine wrote a defense of the doctrine of restoration, that promoted that any Christian could be forgiven of any sin, even the betrayal of their faith and handing over the Scriptures to their persecutors. Augustine's

---

1. Walker, *History*, 100–101.

view was accepted by the majority of Christians and the Donatist sect faded away.[2]

THE ARIAN CONTROVERSY

Another danger to the unity of the Christian church was the Arian controversy. It began in Alexandria in about 320 CE and became a schism that lasted throughout most of the fourth century. The church held a council in Nicaea in 325 to settle doctrinal conflicts. Constantine called this council and he presided over it. The formal doctrine of the Trinity was worked out in this council and expressed in the Nicene Creed. The final statement of the creed was written at the Council of Constantinople in 381 CE. Most Christian churches have the Nicene Creed as a statement of faith of Christianity.[3]

Arius was an elderly preacher held in high repute. He had been influenced by Monarchian teaching in Antioch, which led him to emphasize the unity of God. He followed a teaching that Christ was a created being. Origen declared the eternity of the Logos, the Son, with the Father.[4] Arius went beyond that teaching and for him, Christ was God in a certain sense, but a lower God. He thought of Jesus Christ as the incarnation "not of God but of a great creature of God – the Logos, who had a beginning in time and remained forever subordinate to the Father, not only in terms of his role but also in terms of his very being."[5]

OPPONENTS OF ARIUS

The opponents of Arius, including Bishop Alexander, held to the belief that the Logos is divine and shares God's nature. Yet they struggled to explain the incarnation of the Logos in humanity. Arius declared that the Father was eternal and immutable, whereas the Logos (or Son of God) was created before the world and was capable of changing and suffering.

Over one hundred bishops that gathered in Alexandria in 318 CE, condemned Arius and his teaching about Christ as heresy. They reacted

---

2. Walker, *History*, 106.
3. Olson, *Story of Christian Theology*, 139.
4. Olson, *Story of Christian Theology*, 110.
5. Olson, *Story of Christian Theology*, 142.

so strongly because they saw Arius's heresy as threatening salvation itself. What they believed mattered to them and this heretical teaching threatened to distort the gospel message and to become another religion. The relationship of Jesus to God is very important. In Arianism, the Son of God was said to be pre-existent and he was higher than any other creature. He was said to be a divine being incarnated in a human being. The sticking point was that the Arians taught that Jesus Christ was not equal with God the Father.

ATHANASIUS (C.296-373)

The presbyter of Bishop Alexander was Athanasius (c.296–373), who argued that contrary to Arius's idea that Christ was the highest creature, if Jesus Christ were not truly God, then he could not accomplish redemption. Alexander and Athanasius argued the co-eternity and co-divinity of Jesus and the Father. While the Son had his being from the Father in his incarnation, "he has *eternally* been the Son of the Father. As such he is fully God."[6] They considered Arius to have improperly read the New Testament texts that showed the relationship of the Father and the Son.

OF THE SAME ESSENCE

The ecclesiastical council in Nicaea in 325 CE supported the position of Alexander and Athanasius. It ruled that the Son was *homoousios* — "of the same essence" with God the Father. Only the creator could redeem the created world from its sin. Some of the eastern church leaders did not agree with the *homoousios* statement, as they said if the Father and the Son were of the same essence this could put into question whether they might be the same person. They suggested, with just an addition of an 'i', that "the Son is of an essence "similar to" (*homoiousios*) that of the Father."[7] Although they are sometimes known as Semi-Arian, they did help to clarify the basic trinitarian terms and show that the members of the Trinity could share in the divine essence, but remain distinct persons.

Athanasius was archbishop and patriarch of Alexandria for forty-five years (328–373 CE), although part of that time he was exiled due to his

---

6. Plantinga et al., *Introduction to Christian Theology*, 438.
7. Plantinga et al., *Introduction to Christian Theology*, 439.

defense of the Nicene Creed. He was a great hero of the faith and regarded as one of the great teachers of the early church. He refused to compromise for the sake of unity in the church. Emperors during the fourth century tried to compromise with the Arians, but Athanasius fought for the truth. Soon after the Council of Nicaea, a Sabellian bishop declared that the term *homoousios* (of the same essence) identified the Father and the Son so closely that they could be considered one in identity, and their only difference was in how they manifested themselves.[8]

The Council had not properly explained the distinction between the Father and the Son and where the Holy Spirit fitted in. The Sabellians claimed the Council was a victory for their view of the Trinity and this put the Arians back in a stronger position. There were arguments between bishops and Emperor Constantine. In 332 Constantine restored Arius and tried to persuade Athanasius to accept him back. This Athanasius refused to do unless Arius would accept *homoousios* as affirmed by the Council as describing the relationship between the Father and the Son. Arius would not, and Constantine exiled Athanasius to Trier in Germany.

ATHANASIUS IN EXILE

Even in exile, Athanasius remained for the people of Alexandria their bishop. During this time of exile, Athanasius was well received by many western bishops, and he helped to uphold the Nicene formula for the Trinity in the west. Athanasius was also introduced to the desert Fathers, the ascetic monks living in the Egyptian deserts, and in particular to St Anthony. He wrote a book during this time entitled *The Life of Anthony*, which spread the ideas of monasticism. Arius died in 336 and Constantine in 337.

ATHANASIUS RETURNS TO ALEXANDRIA

Constantine's son Constantius succeeded as emperor and allowed Athanasius to return to Alexandria. Wanting peace and harmony, Constantius decided that the term suggested by the semi-Arians meaning the Father and the Son shared a 'similar substance' should be accepted, instead of the belief that they are of the same substance or being. This would re-open the

---

8. Olson, *Story of Christian Theology*, 163.

door to the Arian interpretation which would imply that the Son is not God in the same way that the Father is.

Athanasius could not support this. He was concerned to support the gospel and could not accept the semi-Arian compromise. Salvation would depend on the Son of God being God, and not just a creature, however great. Jesus must be truly God as well as truly human. The words *homoousios* and *homoiousios*, although just different by one letter, make the difference between the Son being God or being *like* God. This is where the essence of the argument lay and the difference between orthodox Christianity and heresy lay.

Athanasius was faced with trumped-up charges because he would not compromise. He was forced to flee to Rome in 339, and it was some while before he was cleared of the charges and allowed to return to Alexandria. Athanasius was attacked by Roman guards while taking a service in the Cathedral in Alexandria, and it was only the action of the congregation that prevented him from being arrested or even killed and enabled him to slip away. He went to the desert and lived with the desert monks for about six years.

It was largely through the work and dedication of Athanasius and the Cappadocian fathers, Basil of Caesarea, Gregory of Nazianzus, and Gregory of Nyssa, that a statement was proposed that the Father, the Son, and the Holy Spirit were three distinct but not separate *hypostases* of the one God. This Greek word generally meant 'the individual example of a common species.' This idea made clear that the Trinity was of one substance but not the same person. Therefore they were three distinct persons. They had come to the same formula that Tertullian had in his Latin trinitarian formula over a hundred years earlier: *una substantia, tres personae*.

"Though they are not three Gods, they are three distinct relations to one another. The Father is the eternal cause, ground, and source of the Son and the Holy Spirit. The Son is the one eternally begotten of the Father, and the Spirit proceeds from the Father eternally."[9]

THE WORKS OF ATHANASIUS

Athanasius wrote *On the Incarnation of the Word*, and *Four Discourses Against the Arians*. He argued in his book *On the Incarnation of the Word* that Jesus Christ was God. God needed to be incarnated for human beings

---

9. Olson, *Story of Christian Theology*, 193.

to be saved. "For in speaking of the appearance of the Saviour amongst us, we must needs speak also of the origin of men, that you may know that the reason of His coming down was because of us and that our transgression called forth the loving-kindness of the Word, that the Lord should both make haste to help us and appear among men."[10]

The final steps towards the creation of the New Testament took place in the later fourth century. Athanasius produced a list that contained all twenty-seven books from Matthew to Revelation and no others, despite the previous debates over whether the *Didache, Shepherd of Hermas, and Epistle of Barnabas* were worthy of inclusion. Athanasius presented his list in a letter to Christian congregations in Egypt in 367. Two church meetings were held in North Africa in Hippo in 393 and in Carthage in 397, in which Athanasius' list was affirmed as final and which settled the contents of the New Testament.

Athanasius died in 373 in Alexandria. He and the Cappadocian fathers paved the way for the success of the Nicene doctrine of the Trinity. This took place in 381 at the Council of Constantinople.

THE NICENE CREED

An authorized translation of the Nicene Creed is used in some worship services.

> We believe in one God,
> the Father, the Almighty,
> maker of heaven and earth,
> of all that is,
> seen and unseen.
>
> We believe in the one Lord, Jesus Christ,
> the only Son of God,
> eternally begotten of the Father,
> God from God, Light from Light,
> true God from true God,
> begotten, not made,
> of one Being with the Father;
> through him all things were made.
> For us and for our salvation he came down from heaven,

---

10. Athanasius, *Complete Works*, loc. 1036.

was incarnate from the Holy Spirit and the Virgin Mary and was made man.
For our sake he was crucified under Pontius Pilate;
He suffered death and was buried.
On the third day he rose again
in accordance with the Scriptures;
he ascended into heaven
and is seated at the right hand of the Father.
He will come again in glory to judge the living and the dead,
and his kingdom will have no end.

We believe in the Holy Spirit,
the Lord, the giver of life,
who proceeds from the Father and the Son,
who with the Father and the Son is worshipped and glorified,
who has spoken through the prophets.
We believe in one holy catholic and apostolic Church.
We acknowledge one baptism for the forgiveness of sins.
We look for the resurrection of the dead,
and the life of the world to come.
Amen.[11]

STUDY QUESTIONS

1. Discuss the ways the hostility towards Christianity affected the church.
2. Explain the ideas of Arius and how Athanasius defended orthodox Christianity?
3. What were the difficulties faced by Athanasius?
4. What books did Athanasius's list contain for the New Testament?

---

11. Archbishop's Council, *Common Worship*, 173.

PART THREE
Knowing God

Chapter 9

The Trinity

IN THIS CHAPTER, WE introduce the Cappadocian Fathers, Basil of Caesarea, his brother Gregory of Nyssa, and his friend Gregory of Nazianzus. We look at the renewal of the trinitarian doctrine in the thinking of Karl Barth and others, as an interpretive key for Christian theology.

BASIL OF CAESAREA

Basil of Caesarea was born about 330 CE into a Christian family in Cappadocia. His grandmother Macrina was a godly woman, and she took much of the responsibility for raising Basil. His sister, also called Macrina, was an important influence in his life, and she became a nun early in life and influenced Basil and his younger brother Gregory to become monks. While at school in Athens, Basil met and befriended a young man of the same age as himself, called Gregory of Nazianzus, who was also from Cappadocia.

Basil was ordained in 357 and spent time visiting the monks and nuns living in caves and small monasteries in Cappadocia. Having renounced his family's wealth he became an ascetic. This meant he lived a very simple lifestyle and spent much time in prayer. He was made bishop in 370 and continued to stand against Arianism and Sabellianism. He wrote five books against Arianism and traveled widely to persuade as many people as possible to reject it. He worked towards another council that would endorse the gains of the Nicene council, and to this end, he influenced his brother Gregory of Nyssa and his friend Gregory of Nazianzus.

PART THREE: KNOWING GOD

THE HOLY SPIRIT

Veli-Matti Kärkkäinen suggests that one of the reasons that the doctrine of the Spirit has played a greater role in Eastern Orthodox theology is that its roots are in the works of Athanasius, Cyril of Alexandria, and Basil of Caesarea.[1] There has been a resurgence of interest in the third person of the Trinity in theology, as it is realized that the Holy Spirit is of great significance in the lives of Christians. The great eastern teachers taught that it was "by the incarnation of the Logos that humanity was anointed by the Holy Spirit."[2]

One of Basil's books was *On the Holy Spirit*, which greatly influenced the mention of the third person of the Trinity in the revised Nicene creed. For many church leaders, the Holy Spirit had been forgotten or considered of lesser importance than the Father and the Son. He had not been worshipped as God.

Basil's *On the Holy Spirit* was a response to the criticism which he received regarding the words of his doxology, "Glory to the Father, with the Son, with the Holy Spirit" rather than "Glory to the Father, through the Son, in the Holy Spirit." Perhaps we wonder at people criticizing Basil for his prayer. We need to understand that the church was trying to work out the relationship of the Father, the Son, and the Holy Spirit and just how they were related to each other. Despite the reservations that people had, it was the Cappadocians who largely developed the theology of the Holy Spirit.

EASTERN FATHERS FACE NEW HERESIES

The Eastern fathers faced the heresy of Macedonius and the *Pneumatomachoi* ('enemies of the Spirit'). The *Pneumatomachoi* believed the Spirit was a power or instrument of God working in the world, rather than part of the Trinity. This struggle against the *Pneumatomachoi* brought in the *epiclesis* or prayer over the bread and wine during the eucharist, in which the Holy Spirit is invoked. Another change that was brought in was that the Father and the Son were also included in the feast of Pentecost at which the outpouring of the Holy Spirit was remembered. Thus all of the persons of the Trinity could be adored and glorified together.

1. Kärkkäinen, *Pneumatology*, 12.
2. Kärkkäinen, *Pneumatology*, 43.

It was at the Council of Constantinople in 381 that the Nicene-Constantinopolitan Creed was drafted. One hundred and fifty bishops met to affirm that the Trinity was of one substance, uncreated, consubstantial, and eternal. In this, the unity of the Trinity was emphasized. The Spirit was both the giver of life and of salvation through what was known as the divinization of human beings (*theosis*).[3]

A VARIETY OF APPROACHES TO THE HOLY SPIRIT

Since there are a wide variety of different Christian churches, it is fascinating to see the broad range of how the ministry of the Spirit is approached. There is the mystical approach of the Eastern Orthodox and the enthusiasm of the Pentecostal and Charismatic movements that have also influenced the historic Eastern and Western Christian churches. This includes expressions of the Holy Spirit in lively African and South American Christian groups, and renewal in Protestant denominations as well as the Roman Catholic church.

Eastern Orthodox theology draws on the writings of the church fathers of the East. They tend to be 'spirit-sensitive' and very influenced by the presence and work of the Holy Spirit.[4] This does not mean that they have neglected the Father and Jesus. The Holy Spirit is understood to be the one who makes the first contact which is then followed by the revelation of Jesus and the Father. Thus in the Eastern view, each of the members of the Trinity is working together to bring about revelation.[5]

GREGORY OF NYSSA

It was Gregory of Nyssa, Basil's younger brother, who wrote about the sanctifying work of the Holy Spirit in forming the Christian to be like Christ. Gregory was born in 335 CE. He received a good education and became a professor and was later ordained as a bishop in the city of Nyssa. He sets out the reasons why we worship the Holy Spirit alongside God the Father and the Son. "We, for instance, confess that the Holy Spirit is of the same rank as the Father and the Son, so that there is no difference between them

---

3. Kärkkäinen, *Pneumatology*, 45.
4. Kärkkäinen, *Pneumatology*, 68.
5. Kärkkäinen, *Pneumatology*, 69.

in anything, to be thought or named, that devotion can ascribe to a Divine nature."[6]

Gregory of Nyssa beautifully describes the divinity of the Holy Spirit. "If, then, the Holy Spirit is truly and not in name only, called Divine both by Scripture and by our Fathers, what ground is left for those who oppose the glory of the Spirit? He is Divine, and good, and Omnipotent, and wise and glorious and eternal; He is everything of this kind that can be named to raise our thoughts to the grandeur of His being."[7]

KARL BARTH'S RENEWAL OF THE TRINITARIAN DOCTRINE

In the twentieth century, it was Karl Barth (1886–1968), who worked on a renewal of trinitarian doctrine as the interpretive key for Christian theology.

> In giving this doctrine [i.e. the Trinity] a place of prominence our concern cannot be merely that it has this place externally but rather that its content be decisive and controlling for the whole of dogmatics. The problem of the Trinity has met us in the question put to the Bible about revelation. When we ask: Who is the self-revealing God? the Bible answers in such a way that we have to reflect on the triunity of God.[8]

Barth wrote a commentary on Paul's letter to the Romans. He stressed the otherness of God, but this was not to say that God was indifferent or impotent regarding the human situation. He is not too pure to interact with the human world. He hides his face so that he may reveal himself as the world's creator, and he does this in Jesus Christ. It is in Romans 8 that we hear that all things will be made new and there is a radical hope for redemption.

> The whole creation *waiteth for the manifestation of the sons of God*. From this manifestation of redemption, no hair of our head can be excluded. The vast ocean of reality, which now embraces the Island of Truth, subsides and is established so that only Truth remains: the Truth of veritable Reality! Time, immense and vast, from its

---

6. Nyssa, *Select Works*, loc. 9529.
7. Nyssa, *Select Works*, loc. 9529.
8. Barth, *Church Dogmatics*, 1.1/§8-12, 9.

first beginning to its furthest future, is Eternity! . . . It is not some other man that is redeemed, but I myself; not a fragment of me, but I in my totality. I am transformed, renewed, purified, made a participator of the divine nature and of the divine life, with God, by His side, and in Him. This is adoption.[9]

Barth focuses on the cross and resurrection together in *Romans*. Alongside these events is the eschatological future that God is ushering in. Barth is careful to remind us that this future is "achieved through a death — a reminder that the God who 'gives life to the dead' always acts beyond the bounds of the humanly possible."[10]

DIVINE PERSONHOOD

Plantinga et al., suggest that it is helpful to work with several trinitarian models. The first is that of *divine personhood*. That God is personal is accepted, but how it is to be understood in the Trinity is debated.[11]

Karl Barth and Karl Rahner stated the option of one person existent as Father, Son, and Spirit. The trinitarian 'persons' are God's eternal 'modes of being' (Barth) or 'manners of subsisting' (Rahner) with personhood applying only to the one God singularly. This is called the *neo-modal model*. It is easier for us to imagine one person playing three different roles or being in three different modes at the same time than one person being three persons. The difficulty is whether this model has modalistic tendencies and whether there is confusion over the persons.

The *social Trinity* shows that God is three persons with three centers of thought, will, and consciousness. God is like a family or society of persons. The question is how can three distinct persons still be one God? They are all divine and show divine attributes. The relational unity seen in the Father-Son relationship is best seen as a family tie.

Another form is the *perichoretic unity* of persons. The term *perichoresis*, which was introduced by Karl Barth, emphasizes divine unity and distinction of persons. Many theologians see this model as showing the ties of love and life shared by the persons and that they have unity of purpose, fellowship, and love. Perichoresis "is an expression of the dynamic relationality that characterizes not only the inner life of Father, Son, and Spirit but

---

9. Barth, *Romans*, 313
10. Mangina, *Karl Barth*, 16–17.
11. Plantinga et al., *Introduction to Christian Theology*, 130–146.

Part Three: Knowing God

also the life of the Trinity *ad extra* both in human society and within the natural world."[12]

THE CREATOR GOD

The creator God is the Holy Trinity and creation is a trinitarian act. Father, Son, and Spirit are all divine persons who are co-equal and who together constitute the creator God. This relational view of God has helped to provide a more wholesome and community-based model for human beings and their spirituality than the individualistic one in western society.

THE SELF-REVEALING GOD

For Barth, the doctrine of the Trinity derived from the doctrine of revelation, rather than relationality being the controlling factor.

> The question of the self-revealing God which thus forces itself upon us as the first question cannot if we follow the witness of Scripture, be separated in any way from the second question: How does it come about, how is it actual, that this God reveals himself? Nor can it be separated from the third question: What is the result? What does this event do to the man to whom it happens? . . . God reveals Himself. He reveals Himself *through Himself*. He reveals *Himself*. . . God the Revealer is identical with His act in revelation and also identical with its effect. It is from this fact . . . that we learn we must begin the doctrine of revelation with the doctrine of the triune God.[13]

Thus it is clear that God reveals himself not only by what he has created and done in the world but supremely through his Son Jesus and through the Holy Spirit who has been poured out on the day of Pentecost. The doctrine of the Trinity thus lies at the center of Christian theology and is at the heart of the mystery of God. It also lies at the heart of Christian worship as we declare God as Father, Son, and Holy Spirit.

The early disciples held to the tradition of the Hebrew Scriptures as foretold by the prophets that there is one God, and they rejected the

---

12. Buxton, *Trinity*, 97.
13. Barth, *Church Dogmatics*, 1.1/§8–12, 1–2.

worship of many gods. Deuteronomy 6:4–5 was as important to the faith of Judaism as it still is today.

"Hear, O Israel: The Lord our God, the Lord is one.[5] Love the Lord your God with all your heart and with all your soul and with all your strength." *NIV.*

Another strand came into their faith confession, for they confessed Jesus as Lord and creator and head of the church. We see this declaration of Jesus as God in Romans 9:5: "Theirs are the patriarchs, and from them is traced the human ancestry of the Messiah, who is God over all, forever praised! Amen." *NIV.*

Although the Fatherhood of God is mentioned in the Old Testament, this is usually connected with the people of Israel. An example is in Jeremiah 31:20:

"Is Ephraim my dear son? is he a pleasant child? for since I spake against him, I do earnestly remember him still: therefore my bowels are troubled for him; I will surely have mercy upon him, saith the Lord." *KJV.*

It was Jesus who spoke of God's care for his creation and his people, but above all, he spoke of his heavenly father with the Hebrew name *Abba* which is like our version of a father as daddy, and he instructed his disciples to do the same as he taught them to pray. "Our Father who art in heaven . . ." The language of Father and Son have thus become part of the theological language of the church.

THE WORD OF GOD

Early theologians thought deeply about the relationship of Jesus to God. In the second century, the Christian thinkers called 'apologists' used the Greek Philosophical tradition to use the concept of the Word (Greek – *logos*) to show that Jesus was both personal and was with God in eternity. While the Word was from eternity, he came into expression at the creation as God spoke the universe into existence. At the incarnation, the Word appeared in human form as Jesus, or *Yeshua*, which was his Hebrew name meaning 'God saves'. The beginning of John's gospel sets this out very clearly for us in John 1:1–4:

"In the beginning was the Word, and the Word was with God, and the Word was God. [2] He was in the beginning with God.[3] All things came into being through him, and without him not one thing came into being.

What has come into being 4 in him was life, and the life was the light of all people." NRSV.

The third strand is that of the Holy Spirit, who was now evidently present among the people of God since Jesus poured out his Spirit on the disciples on the day of Pentecost. That is not to say the Holy Spirit or *Ruach Hakodesh* in Hebrew is not evident in the Jewish Scriptures. The Holy Spirit became of importance to the church in a personal way as Jesus ascended into heaven, leaving his divine presence with his followers. Thus the Holy Spirit was added to their trinitarian formulation. An example is found in 2 Corinthians 13:14:

"May the grace of the Lord Jesus Christ, and the love of God, and the fellowship of the Holy Spirit be with you all." *NIV.*

GENERATION

The differentiation within the one God is eternal and intrinsic to his nature. The Father, Son, and Spirit constitute this diversity in the one God, and this has been from eternity. Since the Patristic era, theologians have tried to put into words the essence of God. They have used the word 'generation' to speak of the Son generated by the Father. The Son reveals the Father and carries out his will for creation and the redemption of humanity. The word 'procession' is used of the Spirit proceeding from the Father and the Son. He is the divine power who is active in the world and in a personal way leads us into all truth and carries out the divine will of the Father and the Son.

All three members of the Trinity are involved in every way that God is working in the world, and they cooperate in perfect harmony. The Son is the redeemer of humanity and the Father is at work through him. The Son creates the world, and the Spirit is the divine power bringing the world into existence. The Spirit is at work in the redemption from bringing humans to the new birth to taking us to the eschatological resurrection, and much more besides.

AN EASTERN ORTHODOX PERSPECTIVE

An Eastern perspective on the nature of God as *Holy Trinity* is often not taken into consideration in the Western church when the interrelationship between the three persons of the one God is discussed.

The Trinity

Both Gregory of Nazianzus (329–390 CE) and John of Damascus (676–749 CE) offer an insightful understanding of the first centuries of early Christianity regarding the theological understanding of the trinitarian relationship in the Holy Scriptures.

They explain how each person that makes up the Godhead shares equality, while at the same time they each have their unique distinguishing aspects. The Holy Spirit and the Son are intrinsically related in their origin and procession as well as their interaction and influence.

STUDY QUESTIONS

1. Discuss the importance of Basil of Caesarea in the fourth century.
2. Explain the concept of the Word of God.
3. In what way did the ministry of the Holy Spirit come to be understood through Gregory of Nyssa?
4. Explain the term 'procession.'

Chapter 10

The Doctrine of God

As we look at the doctrine of God, this will include a wide spectrum of his attributes and his relationship to his creation. We will look at the Bible and the environment and the community of creation.

GOD AS CREATOR

From the beginning of the biblical account, God is seen as the one who creates all things. The Hebrew name for the first book of the Bible is *bereshit* which in English means 'In the beginning.' An English synonym for beginning is genesis, which is the name given to the first book of the Bible. When this time frame has been established, it is immediately followed by the activity that God did, namely, he created. It is told us what he created, and that is the heavens and the earth. Gordon Wenham suggests that in the Hebrew Scriptures the phrase 'heaven and earth' denotes the whole cosmos or the entire universe.[1]

This idea of God as creator was put into the Apostles' creed as 'Maker of heaven and earth.' In Genesis 1:2 we read the following: "And the earth was without form, and void; and darkness was upon the face of the deep. And the Spirit of God moved upon the face of the waters." *KJV*. The poetry of this verse is often lost in translation, as the Hebrew phrase 'without form and void' is *tohu vavohu*. Victor Hamilton suggests that this parallels the meaning of desert and wilderness or a place of virtual death for anyone who may stray in there.[2] Yet in this wilderness was the Spirit (wind) of God,

1. Wenham, *Genesis 1–15*, 15.
2. Hamilton, *Book of Genesis*, 109.

hovering over the surface of the waters like a powerful, awesome, tempestuous, and raging wind.

THE CREATOR SPEAKS

The scene is now set in the darkness of the deep pre-Adamic world, for God to be the creator by his spoken word. The word is spoken by God, "Let there be . . ." The first thing that God speaks into being is light, and he separates light from darkness, creating day and night. Day has a variety of light in that there is the dawn of the day turning into morning and the twilight of evening turning again into the night. The Jewish festivals, including the weekly Shabbat or Sabbath, all begin in the evening of the day before as the Sabbath lights are kindled, and end in the evening of the following day. Perhaps this is to mirror the start of the creation of the world in darkness and the word spoken by God, "Let there be light."

ORDER IN THE WORLD

God called for a dome in the waters and he called it sky. He gathered the waters under the sky into one place and dry land appeared. He called them seas and earth and said of them that they were good. The earth was now ready for vegetation, including plants and trees bearing seeds and fruit. Birds flew in the air and sea creatures splashed in the water, including the great sea monsters. Every type of living and creeping creature was now found on the earth. Finally, God made humankind in his image, according to his likeness, and they were male and female.

Each time we see God speaking in this way he is also bringing order into his world, beginning with the light that shines and divides the darkness from the light. This theme continues to run right through the whole Bible and is an important part of the redemptive work of Jesus Christ in coming into this world as 'the light of the world.' This opening of the Bible in which God speaks is echoed in the beginning of John's gospel "In the beginning was the Word, the Word was with God, and the Word was God." (John 1:1) *NIV*.

Lodahl suggests that in the book of Hebrews we read that "this creative power of the divine word continues to sustain creation, to call it into being, for God in Christ, 'upholds all things by the word of his power' (Hebrews 1:3)"[3]

CALVIN ON GOD THE CREATOR AND REDEEMER

Calvin (1509–1564 CE) was a French theologian, pastor, and reformer in Geneva during the Protestant Reformation.

He wrote a lengthy book on *The Institutes of the Christian Religion*. In one section he deals with the topic of God as creator and redeemer and our response to him.

> But although our mind cannot conceive of God, without rendering some worship to him, it will not, however, be sufficient simply to hold that he is the only being whom all ought to worship and adore, unless we are also persuaded that he is the fountain of all goodness and that we must seek everything in him, and none but him. My meaning is: we must be persuaded not only that as he once formed the world, so he sustains it by his boundless power, governs it by his wisdom, preserves it by his goodness, in particular, rules the human race with justice and judgment, bears with them in mercy, shields them by his protection; but also that not a particle of light, or wisdom, or justice, or power, or rectitude, or genuine truth, will anywhere be found, which does not flow from him, and of which he is not the cause; in this way, we must learn to expect and ask all things from him and thankfully ascribe to him whatever we receive.[4]

THE BIBLE AND THE ENVIRONMENT

Ronald Simkins, in his book *Creator and Creation*, points out that books published before 1970 contain little information on the Bible's view of the natural created world, although the Bible has many references to it.[5] We have mentioned the story of creation which starts the Bible. Numerous Bible passages describe God using natural images and describe the splendor of the natural world.

---

3. Lodahl, *Story of God*, 51.
4. Calvin, *Institutes*, 4.
5. Simkins, *Creator and Creation*, 1.

It was Lynn White who argued that the modern exploitation of the human environment using technology and science can be traced to the biblical religion. He points to the dominance of humankind over the physical creation, which God planned for their benefit and to rule over. White saw the need for the Christian religious attitude to the environment to be reformed. He saw the theology of St Francis as aiding the idea of nature being designed for the glory of God and not for the wanton consumption of humankind. His essay set theologians thinking about the biblical view of creation and nature. Some theologians argued Christianity is not to be accused as the cause of the environmental crisis, as the causes of this are very complex, not least the rise in world population. However, White did cause people to begin to think deeply about the relationship of humankind to God's created world.

Christians also began to think about becoming more eco-friendly. Very often it has been secular prophets such as David Attenborough, who have warned of the catastrophic dangers to our world and oceans caused by plastics, pollution, and global warming. They have led the way in making us more aware of how much we need to be thinking of caring for our environment and acting before it is too late.

RICHARD BAUCKHAM ON THE COMMUNITY OF CREATION

Richard Bauckham's book *Bible and Ecology: Rediscovering the Community of Creation* is an exploration of how God, humans, and all things living and inanimate in our world intersect and interconnect with each other. He provides a careful study of relevant passages of Scripture from both Old and New Testaments. Bauckham presents the case of the earth as a self-regulating system, but with the underlying understanding that God is creator and humans have a responsibility of care for the environment.

This argument is carefully unfolded, beginning with the criticism that humankind has not fulfilled its stewardship of the earth in the way that it should. Human understanding of the complexities of the natural world is very limited and we do not have the knowledge or power to steward the earth in the way that we should. Technology has already become a powerful force in damaging the global climate. Human stewardship neglects God's involvement with the earth. Nature needs protection from the harm done to it by humans and time is running out for this kind of repair to be applied to the world. Bauckham gives extensive coverage to understanding the human place in creation from Genesis 1. He argues that the scheme of days of creation is spatial rather than chronological in arrangement. Thus the first three days of creation are the creation of the environments of the heavens, the sky, and the land, and the fourth, fifth, and sixth days the creation of the inhabitants for these habitats. Humans are not the climax of creation, as a progressivist understanding would have. Rather an ecological reading of Genesis "stresses the profusion and diversity of living things, and it portrays the creation, animate and inanimate, as an interdependent whole."[6]

"Then God said, "Let us make humankind in our image, according to our likeness; and let them have dominion over [*radah*] the fish of the sea, and over the birds of the air, and over the cattle, and over all the wild animals of the earth, and over every creeping thing that creeps upon the earth." (Genesis 1:26) *KJV*.

"And God blessed them, and God said unto them, Be fruitful, and multiply, and replenish the earth, and subdue it: and have dominion over [*radah*] the fish of the sea, and over the fowl of the air, and over every living thing that moveth upon the earth." (Genesis 1:28) *KJV*.

The Hebrew word *radah* in Genesis 1:26 and 28 must not be interpreted as subdue or have dominion over violently or forcefully, but rather with care and compassion, like a caring shepherd caring for the animals. In Genesis 2 Adam is shown to till the soil with the Hebrew word *avad* consistently translated 'to work' or 'to cultivate' but also containing within it the meaning of 'to serve', with the duty of taking care of it.[7]

Bauckham contrasts a *hierarchical* model of creation with God at the top, humans in the middle, and the non-human creation at the bottom, with the idea of the *community* of creation, where the earth is shared with other living creatures and the environment, and where all offer worship to God. God's rule becomes the model of care in which grace, mercy, and compassion are exercised concerning the created world, and the earth is shared and preserved.

The Scriptural basis for this argument is worked on from Genesis chapter 1 and other passages such as Job 38-39. Job is included as it comes to a resounding conclusion that neither Job nor, by implication, any other human beings, can rule over the world, control animals, stars, or any aspect of what God has created. Psalm 104 reminds us that God's provision of life,

---

6. Bauckham, *Bible and Ecology*, 15.
7. Bauckham, *Bible and Ecology*, 22.

the essentials for existence, food, habitat, and the seasons of the year are all a gift of the creator. We are all part of a cosmic celebration in which all find their place of celebrating the life God gives to them, whether humans, animals or plants, or any other aspect of what God has made.

Apart from praising God, there is also mourning by all of creation for what Bauckham calls 'ecological death.' There has been a partial return to chaos, which turns back the intention of God to provide a good creation. Romans 8:18–23, Jeremiah, Isaiah, Amos, and Hosea are shown to have much to say about the mourning that all of creation is experiencing. A biblical understanding of wilderness and wild animals provides a background to understanding how forests and orchards are viewed in a more positive light. Bauckham develops the vision of Isaiah of the peaceable kingdom, and how Jesus' wilderness experience was an opportunity for him to engage with the non-human sphere, which included Satan, wild animals, and angels.

Bauckham's book concludes with a discussion on what the biblical meta-narrative is, running from creation to new creation. This is seen in sharp contrast with that which dominated the modern era of the West with its idea of progress, and the current version of economic globalization and technology clashing with that of the Islamic meta-narrative. Bauckham highlights the Christological character of the biblical meta-narrative, looking in brief at the cosmic Christ in Colossians and the gospel of John, and climaxing with the cosmic praise made possible by the resurrection of Christ and our reconciliation with God.

This is a valuable discussion of how we can understand our place as human beings in the created world. The arguments are clearly laid out, and it is useful to have a scholarly overview of mainly Old Testament passages, although some New Testament is also included towards the end. This is a welcome addition to the discussion on environmentalism and its place in the mission of the church.

IS GOD MALE?

As we look at the male and female animals and humans that God designed and made, the question emerges as to whether God is male? Certainly, the Bible uses male language about God. The Greek word for God *theos* is male. There are many analogies used for God in Scripture such as father, shepherd, and king. While these were thought to be a suitable model for God,

McGrath suggests that this is not the same as saying God is male, or that God is confined to this model that is drawn from the ancient Near East. God is not a male human being and sexuality cannot be attributed to God, for it is part of the created order.[8]

Mary Hayter looks at certain female analogies that are used to describe God in the Bible.[9] In God's care for the children of Israel, he is said to carry and comfort them as a mother would do in ancient Hebrew culture. Thus God's love and tenderness towards humanity are expressed in the intimacy of motherhood. Hayter shows that some scholars agree it is right to emphasize some female images for God as a balance to the many male metaphors that abound in Scripture, while others do not accept that God's compassion reveals a maternal aspect of his deity.

Sally McFague asks the question regarding what sort of divine love is suggested by this model of God as a mother?[10] She quotes from the third volume of Paul Tillich's *Systematic Theology*, where he points to the mother qualities of giving birth, carrying, and embracing, and the giving of life itself. McFague suggests that one may feel uneasy about Tillich's suggestion, on the basis that the implication is "divine resistance to independence for created being, whereas Western thought has prized its image of independent individuals who are saved one by one, either by their own moral choices or by divine grace."[11]

Hayter argues that the abundance of male imagery in the Hebrew Scriptures "has no significance as an insight into the subject of sexuality in God. The predominance of masculine over feminine imagery is a reflection of the thought-forms of a male-oriented society and not of a male God… The God of Israel is more than any sexual appellation or images that may be used."[12]

If an Old Testament writer was wanting to show the power and authority of God he would draw on masculine imagery, as in the Israelite home it was the father who was the authority figure and not the mother. Hayter also shows that while some theologians, including feminists, teach that God combines male and female characteristics, it is important to note

---

8. McGrath, Christian Theology, 240.
9. Hayter, New Eve in Christ, 22–24.
10. McFague, *Models of God*, 101.
11. McFague, *Models of God*, 101.
12. Hayter, New Eve in Christ, 39.

that to attribute any sexuality to God is a "reversion to paganism." Neither male nor female sexuality can be ascribed to God.[13]

A PERSONAL AND RELATIONAL GOD

Down through the ages people have spoken about God in personal terms such as his love for those whom he has created. The activity of prayer is based on a relationship between God and us. The difficulty that some have raised in this, is that speaking of God in this way puts him on a level with human beings, who are located in some particular place, and God is said to be omnipresent or everywhere at once.

Karl Barth writes that when we ask questions about the being of God we must consider this in terms of his action and working as revealed to us in his Word. "Thus the man who asks about the God who reveals Himself according to the witness of the Bible must also pay heed to the self-revealing as such and to the men to whom this self-revealing applies."[14] Barth further points out that God who reveals himself in the Bible must be known in his revealing if he is to be known. This revealing includes both the work of the Holy Spirit and above all Jesus Christ.

The Christian faith affirms that God is triune – Father, Son, and Holy Spirit. Speaking of God as triune also means that he is in eternal relationship within the three persons of the Trinity. We could call this the social Trinity. Stanley Grenz argues that not only is God in relationship within the Trinity but also he enters into a relationship with creation, which includes his relationship with us.[15]

Christians have often viewed God as a being. He is, however, an uncreated being, and he exists beyond and within the world of created beings. We find in the Old Testament anthropomorphic language about God. This means attributing human motivation, characteristics, or behavior to natural phenomena, or in this case God. This does not mean God is a human being, but it helps us to understand his characteristics that are like our own, for humans are created in his image.

---

13. Hayter, *New Eve in Christ*, 41.
14. Barth, *Church Dogmatics*, 1.1/§8–12, 4.
15. Grenz, *Theology*, 77.

PART THREE: KNOWING GOD
STUDY QUESTIONS

1. How do you understand God as the creator?
2. Explain the place of humankind in creation?
3. What difficulties occur with the use of male language to describe God in the Scriptures?

Chapter 11
The Attributes of God

THIS CHAPTER DEALS WITH the attributes of God as powerful, almighty, and supreme. He is also all-wise and all-seeing and a God of justice. His transcendence, immanence, immensity, love, mercy, grace, and whether he suffers are also under discussion.

GOD AS OMNIPOTENT

Two of the qualities that the Christian faith attributes to God are omnipotence and omniscience. The Nicene Creed includes the words, "I believe in God, the Father almighty . . ."

This points to God as omnipotent. This means all-powerful, almighty, and supreme. People often ask the question, 'If God is all-powerful then why does he not deal with the problems facing our world, including evil and all the bad things that happen?'

It was C.S. Lewis who suggested that God may be omnipotent, but that does not mean that he can do everything. Anselm suggested that because he is divine and holy he does not sin or pervert justice. He does not go against his nature as the holy God.[1]

Writers such as Duns Scotus (1266–1308 CE) and William of Ockham (1287–1347 CE) suggested that God does not act reliably because any external agency causes him to do so. He is free within himself, but he is also grounded by his divine nature. Ockham argued that God was once free to act in any way. This he called the absolute power of God. He made decisions about how he will act, and an order of things based on his loving and divine

---

1. McGrath, *Christian Theology*, 257.

will. This Ockham called the ordained will of God. In this, the power of God is restricted. Having chosen to create the world he sets aside the option not to create the world.[2]

GOD THE OMNISCIENT ONE

Omniscient means all-knowing, all-wise, and all-seeing. He has complete and unlimited knowledge, awareness, and understanding of all things. If God is all-knowing and all-wise, then surely he can have a solution to all things and the power to put in place the solutions needed? The Christian faith believes that God does have this kind of solution, and history is indeed moving towards the goal that God has for his creation when a new heaven and a new earth will be brought in.

God knows all that is knowable in the past, present, and future. He knows all that is going on in the present in all places. He knows what has happened in all of history and before history. He knows what will be and even what might have been, and all that is possible, including the free actions of human beings. Examples of this can be found in Matthew 11 and 1 Corinthians 2.

Matt. 11:20–21: "Then began he to upbraid the cities wherein most of his mighty works were done, because they repented not: [21] Woe unto thee, Chorazin! woe unto thee, Bethsaida! for if the mighty works, which were done in you, had been done in Tyre and Sidon, they would have repented long ago in sackcloth and ashes." *KJV.*

1 Cor. 2:7–8: "But we speak the wisdom of God in a mystery, even the hidden wisdom, which God ordained before the world unto our glory: [8] Which none of the princes of this world knew: for had they known it, they would not have crucified the Lord of glory." *KJV.*

Jesus tells his disciples what will happen in the future when he will be put to death and then rise from the dead and ascend to his Father in heaven. This knowledge rests on his ability to know future events and will help them to believe in his divinity.

John 14:28–29: [28] "Ye have heard how I said unto you, I go away, and come again unto you. If ye loved me, ye would rejoice, because I said, I go unto the Father: for my Father is greater than I. [29] And now I have told you before it comes to pass, that, when it is come to pass, ye might believe." *KJV.*

---

2. McGrath, *Christian Theology,* 259.

The Attributes of God

ALL WISE OR OMNISAPIENT

God is all-wise or omnisapient. By contrast, our wisdom fails because we are sinners. God plans morally perfect ends and he is without blame, for he will bring them to pass.

Some Scriptures follow that tell of the wisdom of God. He has created the heavens and the earth by his wisdom. His wisdom has governed the seasons of the earth, and the seasons of those who govern on the earth. Any wisdom or knowledge that people have is a gift from God. Psalm 104:24 "O LORD, how manifold are thy works! in wisdom hast thou made them all: the earth is full of thy riches." *KJV*.

Proverbs 3:19 "The LORD by wisdom hath founded the earth; by understanding hath he established the heavens." *KJV*.

Dan. 2:20–21: "Daniel answered and said, Blessed be the name of God forever and ever: for wisdom and might are his: [21] And he changeth the times and the seasons: he removeth kings, and setteth up kings: he giveth wisdom unto the wise, and knowledge to them that know understanding:" *KJV*.

Jeremiah 10:12 "He hath made the earth by his power, he hath established the world by his wisdom and hath stretched out the heavens by his discretion." *KJV*.

THE IMPASSIBLE GOD

Greek philosophy, particularly the work of Plato and Aristotle, has also affected the way we view God. The influence of Plato was strong in the patristic era, linking God to the Form of the Good. Later, Aristotle's idea of the divine being as the *unmoved mover* arose. In this concept, God is the static, final cause of all motion in the world. He remains unmoved by or undrawn by creation. This meant that Christians influenced by Greek philosophy thought of God as the impassible one who is unchanging.[3]

Philo believed that God could not suffer or suffer any kind of passion. Anselm of Canterbury was influenced by this idea and said that while we may experience God as compassionate, he does not experience compassion. Aquinas agreed that God is not affected by our sorrows or moved by our misery.

---

3. McGrath, *Christian Theology*, 249.

The problem with the idea of the unchanging God is that to have an emotional commitment of love there must be some measure of change and even suffering. Also, Jesus suffered and died on the cross and he was both God and human. However, God does not change in his being or attributes. He has made ethical commitments or promises that he made freely, and which are an extension of his moral nature. He does, however, change in some respects as he turns from wrath to peace, as he sees the change in us in coming to repentance through our Lord Jesus Christ.

God's changelessness is best understood as his moral faithfulness and his reliability. God is a God of action and he is constantly at work and present in our lives. He does change his way of dealing with people, but he always keeps his promises and remains morally the same.

THE SUFFERING GOD

Martin Luther (1483–1546) developed a theology of the cross in which he contrasted a theology of glory in which is seen God's glory, power, and wisdom in creation, and in which God is hidden in the suffering of Christ on the cross.

In Luther's sermon "A King Arrives" on the First Sunday in Advent, he describes the conduct of Christ as he enters Jerusalem. "His heart is full of sorrow and compassion towards Jerusalem. There is no anger or revenge, but he weeps out of tenderness at their impending doom . . . offers boundless compassion and goodwill."[4] Luther shows the emotion of Jesus Christ and continues to do so through his sermons, including his depiction of Christ on the cross.

TWENTIETH CENTURY THEOLOGIES OF GOD'S NATURE

In the twentieth century, the view that God does not change came under attack from a movement known as process theology. They saw God as involved with creation, and that he is a being among other beings. God was seen by them as the animating or life principle of the world, which may be seen as his body.[5] Paul Tillich said that God is not a being, but 'being

---

4. Luther, *Sermons of Martin Luther*, 35.
5. McFague, *Models of God*, 70.

itself' or the 'ground of being.' According to Tillich, God is the structure that lies behind reality. This idea is sometimes associated with pantheism.

A different proposal came from Jürgen Moltmann, born in 1926, and Wolfhart Pannenberg, (1928–2014) when they "sought to avoid speaking of God as an existing being among other beings. They sensed the importance of the atheist challenge that the traditional view of God was incompatible with human freedom."[6] In his discussion on the future of creation, Moltmann speaks of the transcendence of God the creator. "All the same, the word transcendence can appropriately be used for God's relationships to something else — for his relationship to the world and history. For it allows us to express what God is and what he is like in his relationship to the world and to men and women through the experience of 'the frontier.'"[7] Pannenberg, in his chapter on the creation of the world in Volume 2 of his *Systematic Theology*, argues the importance of our need for fellowship with God. "Apart from God the creature inevitably falls victim to its corruptibility. To survive, it needs fellowship with the eternal God."[8]

We can see that there is a variety of different ideas in the discussion about the nature of God. Whether it is Aristotle's unmoved mover or Pannenberg's observation that we need a relationship with God, all speak of God's relationship to the world. However different they may be to each other, each of them describes God relationally, whether in his relationships as the triune God or his relationship to the world that he has made.

GOD AS TRANSCENDENT AND IMMANENT

God has been spoken of in two contrasting ways, as transcendent and as immanent. His transcendence speaks of his self-sufficiency apart from the world. In every way, he transcends us and is separate from us. He is exalted overall and is holy.

Isaiah, when he entered the throne room of God as recorded in Isaiah 6:1, said, "I saw also the Lord sitting upon a throne, high and lifted up, and his train filled the temple." *KJV*. Isaiah recognized that God is far above all that is earthly.

The other term used of God is his immanence. This refers to ways in which God is with us and close at hand. He cares for us and comforts us.

---

6. Grenz, *Theology*, 79.
7. Moltmann, *Future of Creation*, 2.
8. Pannenberg, *Systematic Theology*, Vol. 2, 135.

Part Three: Knowing God

He is present to the creation and active within it, including in human history. The Old Testament has many references to God being the creator and sustainer of creation through his Spirit.

In Isaiah, we read of the transcendence and immanence of God. Is. 57:15: "For thus says the high and lofty one who inhabits eternity, whose name is Holy: I dwell in the high and holy place, and also with those who are contrite and humble in spirit, to revive the spirit of the humble, and to revive the heart of the contrite." *NRSV.*

Jesus also pointed to God's work in creation, such as Matthew 5:45: "so that you may be children of your Father in heaven; for he makes his sun rise on the evil and on the good, and sends rain on the righteous and on the unrighteous." *NRSV.*

When Paul spoke to the Athenians in Acts 17:23–25, he stressed that God is not far from us and that in him we live and move and have our being.

[23] "For as I passed by, and beheld your devotions, I found an altar with this inscription, TO THE UNKNOWN GOD. Whom, therefore, ye ignorantly worship, him declare I unto you. [24] God that made the world and all things therein, seeing that he is Lord of heaven and earth, dwelleth not in temples made with hands; [25] Neither is worshipped with men's hands, as though he needed anything, seeing he giveth to all life, and breath, and all things." *KJV.*

Paul was showing them that the true and living God does not live in temples and that we cannot serve him as if he needed anything. He is the God who created all and yet is beyond the creation, for all of it is his and he has all rights of rulership over everything in this world.

God is clearly both immanent and transcendent. He is present and active in the world, but at the same time he is not contained by the world, for he is also beyond the universe and the creation that he has made.

We must hold these qualities of God in balance. In our contemporary world, we tend to focus on the immanence of God and forget about his transcendence. Marva Dawn suggests in a book on worship that one of the problems that we face in our time is that "we have become so nonchalant about the Lord of the cosmos."[9]

If we were more aware of the greatness of God and his infinite power, we would spend more of our time praising him as the mighty king of the universe. Many of the Psalms can be used to help us to praise and worship our mighty God.

---

9. Dawn, *Royal "Waste" of Time*, 7.

Psalm 46:1–7 gives us an insight into the transcendence and immanence of God. He is described as our refuge and strength and a present help in trouble. He is evoked as the LORD of hosts who is with us and who is our fortress. When the earth gives way and the mountains are moved into the heart of the sea and the waters are roaring and foaming and the nations are raging, our God is with us and sheltering us safely. Verse 10 of this Psalm gives us the direction of what we should do as we see the mighty works of God. We should be still and know that he is God, even in times of tumult and upheaval. He will be exalted among the nations and in the earth.

Donald Bloesch helps us to see God's relationship to the world. "God is other, but he does not remain other. He is powerful, but he is free to withhold as well as to display his power. God is best described not as Absolutely Other (as in mysticism and existentialism) nor as the Creative Force (as in process thought and New Age religion) but as the majestic Lord and Saviour (as in biblical religion)."[10] God's immanence is best displayed in Jesus who came to live among us to enact the redemptive love of God in the world.

GOD IS SELF-SUFFICIENT

God does not lack anything. He has within himself all that is necessary for his being God. Just a few examples of all that he has in his being are strength, knowledge, love, and beauty. We may share in some of these aspects, but the difference between God and us is that these are qualities he has in abundance and they are intrinsic to his being, while we as created beings have been given these things in varying degrees by God.

Isaiah 40:12–17 gives us an insight into this immensity and power of God.

[12] "Who hath measured the waters in the hollow of his hand, and meted out heaven with the span, and comprehended the dust of the earth in a measure, and weighed the mountains in scales, and the hills in a balance? [13] Who hath directed the Spirit of the LORD, or being his counsellor hath taught him? [14] With whom took he counsel, and who instructed him, and taught him in the path of judgment, and taught him knowledge, and shewed to him the way of understanding? [15] Behold, the nations are as a drop of a bucket, and are counted as the small dust of the balance: behold, he taketh up the isles as a very little thing. [16] And Lebanon is not sufficient

---

10. Bloesch, *God the Almighty*, 24–25.

to burn, nor the beasts thereof sufficient for a burnt offering. ¹⁷ All nations before him are as nothing; and they are counted to him less than nothing, and vanity." *KJV*.

This passage is a series of rhetorical questions that cause us to think of the qualities of God. His hands are described as being so big that he can hold all the water of the oceans and seas in his palm. He marks off the distance of the heavens in the span of his hand, which is the distance between his thumb and little finger. He is powerful enough to hold the scale that weighs all the mountains of the earth. He does not need anyone to instruct him or be his counselor for he has all wisdom and knowledge. He is entirely just and completely enlightened regarding all things. He is all-powerful and has all wisdom.

In comparison to the greatness of God, the nations are like a drop in a bucket or dust on a scale. All nations are as nothing before him, or even less than nothing. This does not mean that God does not care for the nations. Isaiah is showing a comparison between the mighty power of God and the littleness of humanity. God does care, and many passages in the Bible show the extent of his love and concern for his creation.

Psalm 50:1 describes how "The Mighty One, God the LORD, speaks and summons the earth from the rising of the sun to its setting." *ESV*. God is bigger than the vastest distances that humankind can imagine. The world and all its fullness belong to the LORD. This tells us better than anything that he is self-sufficient and does not need anything that we could offer him.

GOD IS INFINITE

God is infinite in every way. He is all-powerful. He is frequently called the Mighty One in the Bible. Psalm 47:2 calls him the Most High. He is the King of all the earth.

In the eleventh chapter of the book of Job, we find a series of rhetorical questions about the infinity of God. Of course, we can never know or find out the deep things of God or even discover his limits, for he has none. If we try to think of what measurements we know, God is always beyond these in his infinity. God has no boundaries on his being or existence, and he does not run out of power.

Job 11:7–9 speaks of his infinite measure that is beyond any measure of height or depth that we can know. ⁷ "Can you find out the deep things of God? Can you find out the limit of the Almighty? ⁸ It is higher than heaven—what can you do? Deeper than Sheol—what can you know? ⁹ Its measure is longer than the earth and broader than the sea." *ESV.*

Psalm 147:5 Great is our Lord, and abundant in power; his understanding is beyond measure. *NRSV.*

The Psalmist who wrote Psalm 147 understood the infinity of God in every aspect of greatness and his abundance of power. In understanding, he is infinite too. The more we come to accept his infinite power and wisdom, the more it should cause us to come before him in worship and praise.

GOD IS OMNIPRESENT

This means that God is everywhere present. He is not limited by space and time. The Psalmist speaks of this in Psalm 139:7–12:

⁷ "Whither shall I go from thy spirit? or whither shall I flee from thy presence? ⁸ If I ascend up into heaven, thou art there: if I make my bed in hell, behold, thou art there. ⁹ If I take the wings of the morning, and dwell in the uttermost parts of the sea; ¹⁰ Even there shall thy hand lead me, and thy right hand shall hold me. ¹¹ If I say, Surely the darkness shall cover me; even the night shall be light about me. ¹² Yea, the darkness hideth not from thee; but the night shineth as the day: the darkness and the light are both alike to thee." *KJV.*

In Psalm 139 we see that it is impossible to escape from God. Even if we fled as far as possible for a human being, we would find God was there. Whether up into the heavens or in the opposite direction down to hell, we would discover that no place is beyond the reach of God. If we could fly with the speed of light we would not be beyond the reach of God. Every part of the cosmos is controlled by him. Even light and darkness are not beyond God, for he created them too.

Isaiah knew that God is everywhere present, as we see in Isaiah 66:1–2. Not only is God present everywhere, but all things have been made by him and belong to him.

¹"Thus saith the LORD, The heaven is my throne, and the earth is my footstool: where is the house that ye build unto me? and where is the place of my rest? ² For all those things hath mine hand made, and all those things have been, saith the LORD: but to this man will I look, even to him that is poor and of a contrite spirit, and trembleth at my word." *KJV.*

The prophet Jeremiah also knew that God is omnipresent and that nothing limits him in space and time. God exists in all of time and even before it, for he existed before he brought into being this created world and universe, and with it space and time. God is neither spatial nor temporal. He is timeless, but he entered our space and time. Jeremiah 23:23–24:

[23] "Am I a God at hand, saith the LORD, and not a God afar off? [24] Can any hide himself in secret places that I shall not see him? saith the LORD. Do not I fill heaven and earth? saith the LORD." *KJV.*

THE ATTRIBUTES OF GOD

Theology speaks of both the essence of God and his attributes. The essence of God refers to the core features of his being. The divine attributes are the expression of his being. His attributes have been described as God's divine nature in relation to the world.[11] Karl Barth used the term the 'perfections' of God to describe his attributes. For Barth, God not only has perfections, but he is also his perfections. Thus the essence of God is reflected in his attributes.

According to older Reformed theology, his communicable attributes include life, wisdom, will, and power. The incommunicable attributes are simplicity, infinity, eternity, and immensity. Under infinity can be included his eternity and immensity.

Karl Barth divided the perfections of God into freedom and love. Under divine love, we see his grace and holiness, mercy and righteousness, patience, and wisdom. God's divine freedom includes unity and omnipresence, immutability and omnipotence, eternity, and glory.

In God's freedom, he chooses to love. He exercises patience and mercy and grace in his holiness. We should not try to single out any of the attributes or perfections of God such as love alone, for in doing so we could easily neglect his holiness, majesty, wrath, justice, goodness and truth, mercy, and grace. God has revealed himself by entering into our world at a particular time in history.[12]

God's love is shown throughout the Bible alongside his other attributes. His love is unconditional and selfless. In all that he does, God seeks the wellbeing of his people. In the Old Testament, the Hebrew word for God's love is often *chesed*. This refers to the loyal and steadfast love of God. He is faithful in all he does, and this includes the covenant promises that

---

11. Bloesch, *God the Almighty,* 40.
12. Bloesch, *God the Almighty,* 42–43.

he has made to his people. Two examples are found in Psalm 106:1 and Lamentations 3:22–23.

Psa. 106:1 "Praise the LORD!

O give thanks to the LORD, for he is good; for his steadfast love [*chesed*] endures forever." *NRSV.*

Lam. 3:22–23 "The steadfast love [*chesed*] of the LORD never ceases, his mercies never come to an end; they are new every morning; great is your faithfulness." *NRSV.*

Like many other Christians before me, I have found God's steadfast love to have been a constant presence in my life. I know about it through reading the Bible, but I have also experienced it in the day to day events of my life and give thanks to God for his love, which is new every morning, as the writer of Lamentations insists in hope, despite the sufferings of those who feel abandoned. Walter Brueggemann writes in his *Old Testament Theology* of the hope, wonder, and gratitude that is expressed by God's people.

> The great triad of steadfast love, mercy, and faithfulness persist. And out of that rich and deep remembering, the community left in Jerusalem knows something different even about the present. It knows that abandonment and alienation might be real, but the God of compassionate fidelity may still be expected in the midst of abandonment.[13]

GOD'S LOVE IN THE NEW TESTAMENT

The love of God is spoken of throughout the New Testament. The Greek word that is used for the love of God is *agape*. This is love that is given although there is nothing in us that commends us to God. Even though we have sinned and turned away from him, he still shows his love for us. This is supremely shown in his sending his Son Jesus to die for us. Many Scriptures illustrate this, but I have chosen two, from Paul's letter to the Romans and the first letter of John.

Rom. 5:8 "But God proves his love for us in that while we still were sinners Christ died for us." *NRSV.*

1 John 4:9–10 "In this was manifested the love of God toward us, because that God sent his only begotten Son into the world, that we might live

---

13. Brueggemann, *Old Testament Theology,* 298.

through him. Herein is love, not that we loved God, but that he loved us, and sent his Son to be the propitiation for our sins." *KJV*.

The Biblical idea of propitiation is that it is God's way of drawing us near to himself. The word *propitio* means to appease, propitiate, or render favorable. God provides every aspect of this action. He draws near and he provides the ground on which humankind is brought near to him. God provides the offering or sacrifice with which humankind appears before God in worship.

That propitiation was brought about by Jesus himself. He is the divine Son of God and he judges humanity, and yet he takes our place before God the Father. He submits himself to the divine judgment and offers himself in sacrifice to God. He thus mediates between God and humanity, and humanity and God. This is how God has dealt with the sinful condition of humanity and opened the way for us to come close to him. This is love indeed.[14]

GOD'S GRACE AND MERCY

These terms speak of the unmerited favor of God given to those who do not deserve his favor. Grace and gift are often linked. In the letter to the Ephesians chapter 2 verses 4–9, the love, mercy, and grace of God are all linked and show the result of that mercy and grace in bringing us into the kingdom of God.

"[4] But God, who is rich in mercy, for his great love wherewith he loved us, [5] Even when we were dead in sins, hath quickened us together with Christ, (by grace ye are saved;) [6] And hath raised us up together, and made us sit together in heavenly places in Christ Jesus: [7] That in the ages to come he might shew the exceeding riches of his grace in his kindness toward us through Christ Jesus. [8] For by grace are ye saved through faith; and that not of yourselves: it is the gift of God: [9] Not of works, lest any man should boast." *KJV*.

Paul's letter to the Romans is rich in revealing to us the grace of God. Romans 3:21–26 includes a discussion about the righteousness of God, his justice, and his glory, and central to these verses is the justification of sinners freely by his grace, through what Jesus Christ has done for us in dying in our place.

---

14. Torrance, *Atonement*, 68–69.

"²¹But now the righteousness of God without the law is manifested, being witnessed by the law and the prophets; ²² Even the righteousness of God which is by faith of Jesus Christ unto all and upon all them that believe: for there is no difference: ²³ For all have sinned, and come short of the glory of God; ²⁴ Being justified freely by his grace through the redemption that is in Christ Jesus: ²⁵ Whom God hath set forth to be a propitiation through faith in his blood, to declare his righteousness for the remission of sins that are past, through the forbearance of God; ²⁶ To declare, I say, at this time his righteousness: that he might be just, and the justifier of him which believeth in Jesus." *KJV*.

Mercy could be understood as the compassion or pity of God towards those who are in a desperate situation. What has landed us in this situation is sin. This is the reason why we stand as a ruined people. God in his mercy came and saved us, even when we were sinners. This is the merciful saving work of God towards those who are unworthy, hopeless, and helpless. He has made a way in sending Jesus to bring us into his kingdom.

In Titus 3:4–7, Paul wrote to Titus about the goodness and lovingkindness of God in saving us by his mercy. He includes the mention of the Holy Spirit given to us by Jesus Christ and thus the means of our renewal and rebirth.

"⁴ But when the goodness and loving kindness of God our Savior appeared, ⁵ he saved us, not because of any works of righteousness that we had done, but according to his mercy, through the water of rebirth and renewal by the Holy Spirit. ⁶ This Spirit he poured out on us richly through Jesus Christ our Savior, ⁷ so that, having been justified by his grace, we might become heirs according to the hope of eternal life." *NRSV*.

GOD AS JUDGE

Many Christians do not want to face the idea of God as a judge. They accept that God is love but do not want to see the other side of the coin.

In Genesis 6–8, we read of God judging the corrupt world of Noah's day and sending the devastating flood which destroyed both humankind and animals, except for Noah and his family and the animals safely in the ark.

When Abraham intercedes before God as he is about to destroy the sinful city of Sodom in Genesis 18:25, he calls God the judge of all the earth. "That be far from thee to do after this manner, to slay the righteous with the wicked: and that the righteous should be as the wicked, that be far from thee: Shall not the Judge of all the earth do right?" *KJV.*

Reading the whole passage, we see that God is indeed a fair judge and knows just who the righteous and the wicked are in each place.

The Psalmists also knew God to be the one who judges on the earth.

Psalm 75:2: "At the set time that I appoint I will judge with equity." *ESV.*

Psalm 75:7: "but it is God who executes judgment, putting down one and lifting up another." *ESV.*

The writer of the book of Hebrews in 12:23 addresses God as judge: "To the general assembly and church of the firstborn, which are written in heaven, and to God the Judge of all, and to the spirits of just men made perfect..." *KJV.*

THE HOLINESS OF GOD

The biblical meaning of holiness is that God is eternally separate from all that is impure. The Hebrew word for holy is '*kavod*' which means separation or uniqueness. One of the key themes in the book of Leviticus is that the holy God is in the midst of his people. We see this at the beginning of the book, in Leviticus 1:1–2.

Verse 2 is one of many verses concerned with the issue of how the people of Israel deal with their sin and impurity so that they can continue to live in the presence of this holy God. The people of Israel are urged to live lives of personal holiness, both outwardly and inwardly, in their devotion to God. The cleansing of sin is done by God, and careful instructions are given to Moses and the people of how they are to be holy people.

"And the Lord called unto Moses, and spake unto him out of the tabernacle of the congregation, saying, ² Speak unto the children of Israel, and say unto them, If any man of you bring an offering unto the Lord, ye shall bring your offering of the cattle, *even* of the herd, and of the flock." *KJV.*

Leviticus 11 delineates which animals may be eaten by the people of Israel.

Leviticus 11:1–2: "And the Lord spake unto Moses and to Aaron, saying unto them, ² Speak unto the children of Israel, saying, These *are* the beasts which ye shall eat among all the beasts that *are* on the earth." *KJV.*

Exodus 31:15 lays out how the Sabbath day must be kept holy. "Six days may work be done; but in the seventh *is* the sabbath of rest, holy to the LORD: whosoever doeth *any* work in the sabbath day, he shall surely be put to death." *KJV.*

God is teaching his covenant people how to be a people set apart and how to keep to his ways. In Isaiah 6:1–5, the prophet has a dramatic encounter with the holy God which enables him to see his uncleanness and that of the people among whom he lives.

"In the year that king Uzziah died I saw also the Lord sitting upon a throne, high and lifted up, and his train filled the temple. [2] Above it stood the seraphim: each one had six wings; with twain he covered his face, and with twain he covered his feet, and with twain he did fly. [3] And one cried unto another, and said, Holy, holy, holy, *is* the Lord of hosts: the whole earth *is* full of his glory. [4] And the posts of the door moved at the voice of him that cried, and the house was filled with smoke. [5] Then said I, Woe *is* me! for I am undone; because I *am* a man of unclean lips, and I dwell in the midst of a people of unclean lips: for mine eyes have seen the King, the Lord of hosts." *KJV.*

One of the seraphim flies to Isaiah with a lump of burning coal taken from the altar with tongs. As he touches Isaiah's mouth he explains that his guilt is taken away and his sin atoned for.

It is the prophets who write extensively about the people of Israel and their covenant relationship with God and look forward to the outpouring of the Holy Spirit and the Torah (God's teachings) written on the peoples' hearts.

Thus we anticipate the new covenant which is established as Jesus is born into the world.

STUDY QUESTIONS

1. What does God's omnipotence mean?
2. What is the Biblical meaning of holiness?
3. How does the wisdom of humankind compare with God's wisdom?
4. Discuss whether God suffers?

PART FOUR
Jesus, Son of God

Chapter 12

The Incarnation of Jesus

WE WILL LOOK AT the incarnation of Jesus, a central topic of discussion in Protestant theology. We discuss the relevance of the Jewish context into which Jesus was born. The work of Thomas Torrance and N.T. Wright on the incarnation is brought into the discussion and the significance of the prologue of John's gospel and the genealogy at the beginning of Matthew's gospel.

WORD AND SON

The titles Word and Son represent the responses of early Christianity as to how Jesus was both divine and human. Associated with these titles is the use of the word *incarnate* to explain that the Word of God or the Logos assumed human form while remaining the second person of the Trinity. As a result of the incarnation, Jesus Christ has the properties of two natures.

In Protestant theology, the incarnation is a central topic of discussion. Particularly the Lutherans discussed what the incarnation of the Logos meant for his divine and human attributes.[1] A suggestion that came out of these discussions has become known as the *kenosis* theory. This is based on the great Christological hymn of Philippians chapter 2. In verse 7 we read "but emptied himself, by taking the form of a servant, being born in the likeness of men." What does it mean that he emptied himself? Some argued that at the incarnation the Logos divested himself of the divine attributes that were not compatible with human existence. Others said the Son laid aside all divine attributes. I would argue that the Logos did not lay aside the

1. Grenz, *Theology*, 306.

divine attributes or the powers of divinity but gave up the independent exercise of these powers. He submitted to the will of the Father and the Spirit.

JESUS BECOMES A HUMAN BEING

What an astonishing thing that God should become a human being. How amazing that Jesus Christ would leave the glory of heaven. Mary was willing to be God's servant and to bear God's Son as the Holy Spirit overshadowed her. God was prepared to enter into the limitations of earthly life, beginning as we all do, as a baby. He would become dependent on a young girl to care for him and live a human childhood in the home of Mary and Joseph. He would become an adult in a poor village, where much was scarce and danger was constant. Jesus often spoke of the poor and our responsibility towards them. He could do so from his own experience. He would learn to worship and pray as we do and develop a special relationship with his heavenly Father.

THE JEWISH CONTEXT OF JESUS

Roni Mechanic, in his book *A Quest for The Jewish Jesus*, shows the historic context into which Jesus was born.

> Most Jewish and Christian scholars agree that the historical Jesus of the first century was a Galilean Jew. His mother was Jewish, his Jewish followers called him "Rabbi," he spoke Aramaic, quoted the Hebrew Scripture in his teachings and he taught in the synagogue in Galilee and the Jewish Temple in ancient Jerusalem. His Hebrew name was Yeshua (God saves). Also, almost all of his early followers were Jews. So how did we get from the Jewish Jesus of Nazareth of the first century of the common era to the Gentile Christian Jesus of today? Jewish people say, "look at what they have done to him — We don't recognize him at all — he does not appear to be a Jewish person." Yet, Rabbi Leo Baeck says, "He was a Jew among Jews; from no other people could a man like him have come forth and in no other people could a man like him work; in no other people could he have found the apostles who believed in him.[2]

---

2. Mechanic, *Quest*, 3.

The Incarnation of Jesus

CONTINUATION OF ISRAEL'S HISTORY

In approaching this topic, it is important to realize that we are dealing with a historical continuation of the history of the people of Israel. Gabriel Fackre has emphasized the telling of the story of Jesus Christ as 'from before' or with an appreciation of the history of the people of Israel in relationship to God. This story and history come before the birth of Jesus and it paves the way for his coming.[3]

Jesus, or Yeshua as he was called, was first and foremost a first century Galilean Jew, born of a Jewish mother, who in her day would have been called Miriam. The story of his earthly birth is dependent on the Spirit of God or '*ruach*' in Hebrew. In chapter 10, when we discussed the doctrine of God, we looked at the Spirit of God hovering over the surface of the waters in the creation narrative of Genesis 1:2 to bring forth the heavens and the earth through God's breath. In Matthew 1:18–23, we read of the action of the Spirit of God in bringing about the miracle of the conception of Jesus.

[18] " Now the birth of Jesus Christ took place in this way. When his mother Mary had been betrothed to Joseph, before they came together she was found to be with child from the Holy Spirit. [19] And her husband Joseph, being a just man and unwilling to put her to shame, resolved to divorce her quietly. [20] But as he considered these things, behold, an angel of the Lord appeared to him in a dream, saying, "Joseph, son of David, do not fear to take Mary as your wife, for that which is conceived in her is from the Holy Spirit. [21] She will bear a son, and you shall call his name Jesus, for he will save his people from their sins." [22] All this took place to fulfill what the Lord had spoken by the prophet: [23] "Behold, the virgin shall conceive and bear a son, and they shall call his name Immanuel" (which means, God with us)." ESV.

Thus it was the Spirit of God who brought about God's gift of his Son in the womb of Mary, who said 'yes' to God. Twice Matthew stresses that the Holy Spirit caused Mary to be with child. In Luke's gospel, he adds that 'the Most High' would overshadow her. This adds a trinitarian slant to the conception of Jesus as a human being. This is the continuation of God's redeeming activity in human history.

---

3. Fackre, *Christian Story*, 101.

Part Four: Jesus, Son of God

TORRANCE ON THE INCARNATION

Thomas Torrance brings a discussion on the relation of Christ to history in his book on the incarnation. The fact that God has become a human in the historical Jesus is a historical fact, for Jesus is a human. He argues that the fact that *God* became a man "is an event that cannot be appreciated by ordinary historical science, for here we are concerned with more than simply a historical event, namely with the act of the eternal God."[4] This kind of becoming can only be perceived as an eternal act through faith.

Revelation, he argues, is not divorced from history, but is the way that we can recognize God's acts in history. It is important to hold together the historical and theological aspects concerning Jesus Christ, not only in respect of his conception but also regarding his life and ministry. "If the two are not held together, we have broken up the given unity in Christ into the historical on the one hand, and the theological on the other, refracting it into elements which we can no longer put together again."[5]

Torrance argues that we have to start with the 'indissoluble union' of the historical and theological which we find in Christ. This mystery of Jesus as true God and true man is what we have to affirm as we look at his person and work. This encounter of faith with Jesus between us and him is a gift of grace from God, in which we develop a relationship with him and get to know him. Through the Holy Spirit, God gives us not just a historical fact, but the full meaning that Jesus is the living Word of God, the Word made flesh.[6] The incarnation of Jesus is an astonishing claim. That Jesus was God made man and that he took on humanity without losing his deity is a mystery and something to rejoice in. For some, this is a stumbling block that prevents them from believing not only the virgin birth but also the miracle accounts in the Bible, the significance of Jesus' death on the cross, and the resurrection. This being the case, then nothing is left of Christianity, for Jesus has been reduced to a mere man, however remarkable.

JOHN'S PROLOGUE TO HIS GOSPEL

The famous Prologue of John's gospel, John 1:1–18 is often read at Christmas time. Verses 1–5 introduce Jesus as the Word of God. Not only was

---

4. Torrance, *Incarnation*, 5–6.
5. Torrance, *Incarnation*, 7.
6. Torrance, *Incarnation*, 13.

The Incarnation of Jesus

he with God but John clearly states he was God and was with God in the beginning, creating all things and bringing life.

¹ "In the beginning was the Word, and the Word was with God, and the Word was God. ² The same was in the beginning with God. ³ All things were made by him; and without him was not anything made that was made. ⁴ In him was life; and the life was the light of men. ⁵ And the light shineth in darkness; and the darkness comprehended it not. "*KJV.*

John lays out for us the importance of the Son of God's divinity right at the beginning of his gospel account. He calls Jesus the Word. God's Word in the Old Testament flags up for us his creative utterance. It takes us back to Genesis 1 as God says, "Let there be… and there was." God is at work through his Word. All things were made through him. This is *the* Son of God. There is only one person that it refers to and that is Jesus.

This Word of God now becomes flesh as a real human baby. He is still fully God but he fully enters into what it means to be human and to feel every physical sensation and emotion of what it is to be human. The writer of the book of Hebrews in chapter 2 verses 14–18 writes of the significance of his becoming fully human.

¹⁴ "Forasmuch then as the children are partakers of flesh and blood, he also himself likewise took part of the same; that through death he might destroy him that had the power of death, that is, the devil; ¹⁵ And deliver them who through fear of death were all their lifetime subject to bondage. ¹⁶ For verily he took not on him the nature of angels; but he took on him the seed of Abraham. ¹⁷ Wherefore in all things it behoved him to be made like unto his brethren, that he might be a merciful and faithful high priest in things pertaining to God, to make reconciliation for the sins of the people. ¹⁸ For in that he himself hath suffered being tempted, he is able to succour them that are tempted." *KJV.*

This passage makes clear that he shares in our flesh and blood, and therefore he who is life must face death. He does this to destroy the one who has the power of death, and that is the devil. This action of his also frees us from the fear of death that has held us as slaves up to this point in time. He can help us when we are tempted or tested and we think about what he has done for us. Jesus has been through testing and temptations in his life and he offers us his help when we face them in our lives. Most importantly, he has made an atonement for our sins and opened the way for us to enter into the presence of almighty God, following him who is our pioneer, who has gone ahead of us.

PART FOUR: JESUS, SON OF GOD

GLORY UNVEILED

Tom Wright, in his book *How God became King*, writes about the beginning of John's gospel and how the creator becomes part of his creation.[7] He incorporates this into the story of Israel and how God has pitched his tent to dwell amid the Israelites. First, he came to live in the wilderness tabernacle and then in the Jerusalem temple, which both signified the presence of the holy God in the presence of his people. There was always the promise of God's ultimate deliverance, despite the destruction of the temple by the Babylonians in 587 BCE.

John writes of this promise being made good in Jesus. "The Word became flesh and . . . set up among us his '*skene*', his 'tent.'"[8] The Greek word *skene* echoes the Hebrew word *shakan* which means dwell or abide and is the word from which we get the name Shekinah or abiding divine presence of the glory of God.

THE CREED AND THE CANONICAL GOSPELS

As we move from the incarnation of Jesus to his later life and look at the gospels, we find a problem with what is included in the great creeds.

> The great creeds, when they refer to Jesus, pass directly from his virgin birth to his suffering and death. The four gospels don't. Or to put it the other way round, Matthew, Mark, Luke, and John all seem to think it's hugely important that they tell us a great deal about what Jesus did between the time of his birth and the time of his death.[9]

One of the twentieth century's most influential German Lutheran New Testament scholars, Rudolf Bultmann (1884–1976), did not include the story of Jesus as drawn from the gospels as part of New Testament theology. For him, all that was needed was the fact of Jesus' death on the cross and "the early church's reflection on the meaning of the cross."[10]

I think that the gospel accounts of the life of Jesus are vitally important in our grasp of theology. Between his birth and his death, there is a wealth of material that helps us to understand who Jesus is and what he has done.

7. Wright, *How God became King*, 101.
8. Wright, *How God became King*, 102.
9. Wright, *How God became King*, 11.
10. Wright, *How God became King*, 21.

The Incarnation of Jesus

We become better disciples if we read the gospel accounts of what he taught and how he responded to people in compassion and healing love.

STUDY QUESTIONS

1. What do you understand by the incarnation of Jesus?
2. Discuss the relevance of the Jewish context into which Jesus was born.
3. How do you understand the *Kenosis* theory?
4. What does the prologue of John's gospel set out to achieve?

Chapter 13

Walking with Jesus

WE WILL NOW CONSIDER some aspects of the life and ministry of Jesus. The importance of his prayer life and his transfiguration show his connection with his heavenly Father. The significance of the exodus, the Passover celebration, and his entry into Jerusalem set the scene for the next chapter on his suffering, death, and resurrection.

FOUR GOSPELS

The life of Jesus between his birth and his crucifixion is a vitally important part of the story of God and deserves to be looked at and studied in great depth. We have four gospels telling us about the life of Jesus and all his teaching, miracles, controversies with his opponents, and details of his family and his ministry, culminating in his death and resurrection and ascension into heaven.

Each of the evangelists tells the story of Jesus in their own way, although the synoptic gospels Matthew, Mark, and Luke often repeat the stories or sayings of Jesus. They see the story of Jesus' life as the climax of Israel's story.

MATTHEW'S GOSPEL

Matthew begins his gospel with the genealogy or family tree of Jesus, going back from Abraham to David is fourteen generations, from David to the exile in Babylon in another fourteen generations, and from the exile to the Christ (Greek – *Christos* meaning 'anointed': compare the Hebrew

– *mashiach*) in another fourteen generations. Names and family links were important to Jewish people in those days, for they established a person's lineage and inheritance rights. Ancestry was also linked to the covenants that God made with Israel.

In talking about Jesus Christ, it is not long before Matthew is pointing out the virgin conception of Jesus and the significance of his name Yeshua meaning 'God saves.' Matthew indicates that the angel is telling Joseph that this is the one who will save his people from their sins. All this has been spoken of by the prophet Isaiah, whom Matthew quotes in 1:23:

[23] "Behold, a virgin shall be with child and shall bring forth a son, and they shall call his name Emmanuel, which being interpreted is, God with us." *KJV.*

Matthew is pointing to Jesus as the one who will end Israel's exile because he is God with us.[1]

JESUS ANNOUNCES THE GOOD NEWS.

In Mark 1:14-15, Jesus announces that the Kingdom of God has arrived. God's power to save his creation is here.

[14] "Now after that John was put in prison, Jesus came into Galilee, preaching the gospel of the kingdom of God, [15] And saying, The time is fulfilled, and the kingdom of God is at hand: repent ye, and believe the gospel." *KJV.*

God is acting through Jesus in love and power to restore and save his creation, and this is the good news. All of humankind can now live under the reign of God as they follow Jesus. He is calling them to give up their false notion of the world and embrace the reality and presence of God, which is found in him. It begins with repenting, which is turning away from the old life and turning to him to teach them the new life. A rabbi would teach his followers about the Torah or teachings of God. Jesus was calling them to give up the old life and learn to live as he did and to learn about him and give him their full devotion. This is really what living in the kingdom of God is all about.

---

1. Wright, *How God became King,* 71.

PART FOUR: JESUS, SON OF GOD

THE MIGHTY WORKS OF JESUS

You only have to start reading your way through the gospels to see Jesus healing those who are sick with every kind of disease and affliction, whether caused by pain, demonic oppression, paralysis, or epilepsy.[2] Jesus cleanses a leper, and in that day it would mean this man's life in the community was renewed too, and his ability to work and live life to the full.[3] Jesus is also reaching out to people outside the Jewish faith. He heals the servant of the Roman Centurion.[4] By his word, he casts out demons who are oppressing many and heals those who are sick. Matthew related these events that he witnessed as a fulfillment of what was spoken in Isaiah 53:4. The strongholds of the spirit world were being invaded and overpowered as Jesus, God's only Son, showed up. Even the demons in the two men they encountered in Gadara, southeast of the Sea of Galilee, recognized who had come and begged to be allowed to enter the large herd of about two thousand pigs, and promptly the herd rushed down a steep bank and into the sea, where they were drowned.[5]

JESUS PRAYS

In the gospels we see Jesus inundated with sick and demon-possessed people clamoring for his attention and hoping for the healing that they needed. Jesus needed time to pray and commune with his heavenly Father, and he would find that solitude early in the morning in a place where he could be alone and pray.[6] We read that at times he prayed all night.[7] Not only does this tell us of the importance to Jesus of having time to spend time alone with his heavenly Father, but it was also the key to the working of the Holy Spirit in and through him.

2. Matthew 4:23–25
3. Matthew 8:1–4
4. Romans 8:5–13
5. Mark 5:13
6. Mark 1:35
7. Luke 5:16 and 6:12

JESUS MULTIPLIES THE LOAVES AND THE FISHES

Matthew 14:13–21 tells the story about the multiplication of the loaves and the fishes. Most of us could probably tell the story at once without much effort at remembering it. It is one of those stories that has been retold so many times, and it warms our hearts to think of Jesus feeding the people gathered to listen to him teach. Some stories are only told once in the gospels, but this one is told four times. It is the only gospel miracle that is told in its fullness in all the gospels. Perhaps it is so popular because it tells us about what Jesus was like. It tells us about his disciples and shows us the love and generosity of God as the one who provides our daily food and uses us to help others who need their daily food too.

As we read the chapter in which this story is situated, it takes on a slightly different appearance. The cousin of Jesus, who was John the Baptist, had been brutally beheaded by the command of Herod, and when Jesus heard the news he needed to withdraw from the world for a bit and find a private and solitary place where he could deal with his feelings of grief. He climbed into a boat to sail across the Sea of Galilee to a remote point.

The Sea of Galilee is fed by the Jordan River, rainfall, and springs on the northern side. More properly designated a lake, the Kinneret (the Old Testament and modern name) is thirteen miles long and seven miles wide. At its deepest point, the lake is only one hundred and fifty feet deep. Jesus loved to be out on the Sea of Galilee and alone with his disciples, and being fishermen they would have done the rowing.

There are times when we need space and time to reflect on what has happened. For Jesus, there was hardly any time for him to do this, and soon crowds of people were invading his privacy and coming with their sick loved ones for him to touch and heal. Jesus was still in the boat and coming to land at this solitary place when a large crowd had already gathered. What was his reaction? He could have said please go away, this is my time for quiet and space. But he did not.

Matthew tells us that when Jesus landed and saw a large crowd, he had compassion on them and healed their sick. We see Jesus' innermost feelings and character being shown here. He had compassion for the poor and the sick. Desperate people came looking for him. He had the power to heal them from their sicknesses and disabilities and he willingly responded to their desperation and reached out in his great love to touch, heal, and set them free. We know that he viewed these people as helpless and like sheep without a shepherd. He saw himself as the Good Shepherd and fulfilled the role of caring for people in every way that a good shepherd would care for his or her sheep. When sick they would need to be nursed. When hungry they would need to be fed.

This of course leads us into the next part of the story, when the evening is approaching and the disciples want him to send the crowds away to the villages to buy themselves food. Jesus turns this around and says that they don't need to go away. He tells them that they must give them something to eat. Was Jesus testing them? Perhaps he was seeing if they would do what most of us do and try to solve life's problems ourselves. They showed themselves to be very human. They responded that they only had five loaves of bread and two fish.

In this story, there is no rebuke for the short-sighted disciples. Only a command to have the loaves and fish brought to him. Also directions about how to seat about twenty thousand people on a hillside in an orderly way. The word used for sit is one used for reclining on couches and would imply that this was to be a formal meal or banquet. Perhaps it was meant to be a foretaste of the future heavenly banquet.

God is never fazed by large numbers of people. He knows what is going on with each of us, every moment of every day and night. He desired to feed each one with an amazing and miraculous provision of bread and fish. The start of the meal was with Jesus taking the seven loaves and the fish, giving thanks with a typical Jewish blessing, breaking them, and then giving them to the disciples to give out to the people. All ate and had more than enough. There were twelve large baskets of leftover food when all had eaten. Most of the crowd were probably unaware of where the food came from, but the disciples who handed it out certainly knew that this was miraculous food.

I am sure that the people who ate the food that Jesus miraculously provided would have enjoyed the smell of the freshest and crustiest bread you can imagine and the freshest and tastiest fish you have ever tasted. This was heavenly food given for people to enjoy as well as to sustain them.

The Psalmist in Psalm 104:14-15 picks up on this delight of God's created world:

> [14] "He causeth the grass to grow for the cattle, and herb for the service of man: that he may bring forth food out of the earth; [15] And wine that maketh glad the heart of man, and oil to make his face to shine, and bread which strengtheneth man's heart. " *KJV.*

When we reflect on this story, I am sure that each one of us would find something different that strikes us. Jesus used what was given to him and turned it into a blessing for many hungry people. He showed that our faith is also intensely practical. He healed and taught the people, but he also made sure that their physical needs were met and did not leave that to others, even to his disciples. Only he could feed that number of people from such a meager offering.

He also shows us that whatever we give to him, however small it is, will be transformed into something else by his love and power. We probably don't see ourselves as being up to much, but that is beside the point. God wills us to give our hearts, our lives, our skills, and all that we have and are, to him. This story assures us that God will take that little bit that is us and multiply and transform our offering for the extension of his kingdom and the blessing of other people.

Perhaps this story tells us that good food is the gift of God, and with tastes as diverse as soft white rolls, Italian ciabatta bread, fresh French bread, fish, meat, fruit, salad, vegetables, . . . the list goes on and on. How thankful we should be for the variety of foods that God has given us to enjoy!

During this time of lockdown due to the Covid-19 virus, my husband and I have been growing salad leaves, tomatoes, courgettes, spinach leaves, and garden herbs. It has given us much pleasure to be able to go into the garden and pick fresh food and give thanks to God for his wonderful provision and bounty.

This story also tells us that when we give our gifts to God and pray, that he will use them. He is more than able to do some miraculous multiplication. Our hearts given to God will be transformed from human selfishness and self-seeking to a generous outlook on life and the miracle of living in Christ.

Jesus validated his claim to be the Messiah of God's kingdom in so many ways and miraculous acts that reveal God's saving power and love at work in him. We would do well to read the gospels again and again and learn much of what they have to tell us about Jesus and his life, and what our response can be in following him. The wonderful liberating power of God is seen working through Jesus as he calms the storm on Lake Galilee and saves his disciples from drowning, and as he raises Lazarus and Jairus' daughter from death. We are given a glimpse into what it is to live in the kingdom of God, renewed and set free from sickness and pain and death itself and finding ourselves in the biblical story.[8]

TRANSFIGURATION

Maybe the word transfiguration is not used in everyday language. It describes an even bigger change that takes place than the word transformed. A definition could be, 'a complete change of form or appearance into a more beautiful or spiritual state.' Exodus 34:29–34 tells the story of Moses when he went up Mount Sinai with two newly cut stone tablets to receive the law from God. If you wanted information to last then you would chisel it into stone.

This was a big event in the life of God's people. God was going to give them the framework to live as his people. God had promised to show Moses his glory, and so when Moses was up the mountain and God descended on it in a cloud he hid Moses in a cleft of a rock and proclaimed his glory as he passed by, allowing Moses to see the afterglow of his presence. For mortals to see the full impact of the glory of God would kill us. Moses saw just a little of God's glory and even that transformed his face to glow with the light of God. Israel first saw the glory of God when they left Egypt and headed for the Red Sea. The LORD went ahead of them by day in a pillar of cloud to guide them on their way, and at night in a pillar of fire so that they could travel by day or by night. This must have been a spectacular sight.

No wonder the people were afraid when they saw Moses's face shining as he came down the mountain with the commandments written on the stone tablets. Perhaps seeing Moses's face like that reminded the people of the glory and judgment of God. So Moses veiled his face when he came down from visiting God the next time. In time the glory of God faded from the face of Moses.

The ministry of the Holy Spirit constantly exposes people to God's glory and his transforming power. This ministry is greater than that of Moses. Ezekiel wrote that God would give us a new heart and put a new spirit within us. God would remove our heart of stone and give us a heart of flesh so that we could obey him.

---

8. Bartholomew and Goheen, *Drama of Scripture*, 107.

THE TRANSFIGURATION OF JESUS

Luke 9:28–36 tells us about the transfiguration of Jesus. He took Peter, James, and John up the mountain to pray. As Jesus was praying, his face changed, and his clothes became as bright as a flash of lightning.

As we read of Jesus' face changing and his clothes glowing brightly we are surely reminded of Moses when he went up the mountain of God. Yet we know that the transformation of Jesus was greater than that of Moses, and was a true transfiguration. Jesus' disciples saw this transfiguration take place before their very eyes. It was as if the veil of his humanity was lifted and his true essence shone through. The glory of his divinity rose to the surface and his friends had a preview of his future glory.

What about the other figures that they saw talking to Jesus — Moses and Elijah? They were talking about his departure which would happen in Jerusalem, more specifically his impending death, resurrection, and ascension into heaven. Why Moses and Elijah? Moses was the lawgiver and Elijah was the great prophet. Jesus was the fulfillment of everything that the law pointed to and that the prophets prophesied about. He fulfilled every prophecy of the Messiah.

What an amazing sight that must have been as the luminous, dazzling Jesus spoke to Moses, who had been dead for over one thousand four hundred years, and Elijah, who had been gone for about nine hundred years. One would think that an experience like this would cause one to be speechless. But not so Peter. He wanted to make special tents for the heavenly visitors so that they could preserve that special moment forever. Peter was confused. He had put all three — Jesus, Moses, and Elijah on a level. Jesus chose not to answer him, but there was an answer from heaven.

Luke 9:34–35: "While he [Peter] was speaking, a cloud appeared and covered them, and they were afraid as they entered the cloud. [35] A voice came from the cloud, saying, 'This is my Son, whom I have chosen; listen to him.'" *NIV.*

They were commanded by God to listen not to Peter but Jesus. Jesus is a greater authority than Moses or Elijah the prophet or anyone else. He is the Son of God.

Part Four: Jesus, Son of God

CELEBRATING THE PASSOVER

For Israel, the greatest of all acts of God's redemption was when he delivered the children of Israel from her bondage in Egypt under the leadership of Moses. God raised up Moses to set his people free from their slavery and oppression in Egypt. God prepared the way for their deliverance and their eventual entry into the promised land of Canaan. The exodus was a happening in history that was retold and retold down through the years, shaping the identity of Israel and providing hope for the future. This memory of the great event was kept alive in a ceremony that was to be undertaken every year.

The exodus would be remembered, and God's faithfulness and loving kindness would be celebrated in the Passover celebration. This was a celebration for seven days, in which the deliverance from Egypt was to be remembered, and only unleavened bread was to be eaten because they came out of the land of Egypt with such haste that the bread did not have time to rise. The Passover lamb was also a symbol of this feast, and later wine and other elements were added to tell the story.

Central to this festival is the mighty deliverance that God did among his people. Not only did he want them to know this, but also all nations of the earth. This could be expressed as the mission of God throughout the Old Testament and then through Jesus.

"Whether through the experience of God's saving grace or exposure to God's righteous judgment, Israel came to know who the true and living God is. And by the same means, ultimately, the nations too will come to know his identity, either in repentance, salvation, and worship or in defiant wickedness and destruction."[9]

Chris Wright sets out all the things that God is wanting Pharaoh to learn in Exodus 7–14, in which the story of his dealing with Egypt is unfolded.[10]

"The Egyptians will know that I am the LORD." (Ex. 7:5, 17)

"So that you may know there is no one like the LORD our God." (Ex. 8:10)

"So that you will know that I, the LORD, am in this land. (Ex 8:22)

---

9. Wright, *Mission of God*, 122.
10. Wright, *Mission of God*, 94.

"So that you may know that there is no one like me in all the earth." (Ex. 9:14)

"I have raised you up for this very purpose, that I might show you my power and that my name might be proclaimed in all the earth." (Ex 9:16)

"I will bring judgment on all the gods of Egypt. I am the LORD." (Ex. 12:12)

"The Egyptians will know that I am the LORD when I gain glory through Pharaoh, his chariots and his horsemen." (Ex. 14:18)

The Egyptians will be forced to acknowledge that the God of Moses is truly God and that he has no rivals. He is God in Egypt and throughout the world, and he is the judge of those who oppose him and deliverer for those who worship and obey him.

The people gathered each year to celebrate the Passover and to give thanks to God for his mighty power. They traveled from all over the country to be present at the temple in Jerusalem for this special celebration. For some, it may have been an experience of a lifetime, for others a yearly pilgrimage. It was a time of great excitement, as all celebrations should be. This was a celebration of God's deliverance of his people from the land of Egypt and their slavery there. Every year this story was told, how God had saved his people through the waters of the Red Sea by the leadership of Moses and by many miracles of God's divine intervention.

This year word had leaked out that Jesus was on his way to Jerusalem. He was known widely for his preaching, healing and miracles, and the raising of Lazarus from the dead. As a result, Jesus had a following of people who had seen him do this miracle and who continued to spread the word about what they had seen.

Jesus' raising of Lazarus from the dead was the culmination of his healing ministry. It was also the cause of harsh opposition on the part of the temple leaders and ardent following on the part of those who had seen the awesome event and believed in Jesus as a result. It was an event that seemed to open the gulf between his opponents and supporters wider than ever. They had seen a public example of his ministry of giving life to the dead. It showed people that this is what he promised to all those who believed in him.

Part Four: Jesus, Son of God

The raising of Lazarus was considered a miraculous sign. It was one of the seven signs in John's gospel that showed that Jesus was the Messiah for whom all Israel was waiting. When people heard that he had performed this sign, they went out to meet him. They formed a jubilant procession. They cut branches off the palm trees growing at the side of the road. Even before he came towards the city they were waving the branches in anticipation and shouting *Hosanna* – Lord save us. They were greeting the one whom they were sure would save them from the oppressive rule of the Romans. He was coming to Jerusalem to be crowned king and lay claim to the throne of David.

They blessed him — the Messiah who came in the name of the Lord. They gave him the unique title King of Israel. This was not the first time that they had wanted to make him their king. Previously he had avoided the crowd and hidden away. Now he was entering the city because he knew this was the appointed time for the culmination of his life's work.

He came on a young donkey, in fulfillment of a prophecy from Zechariah 9:9 that speaks of the coming of the ruler of God's people as follows:

> "Rejoice greatly, O daughter of Zion; shout, O daughter of Jerusalem: behold, thy King cometh unto thee: he is just, and having salvation; lowly, and riding upon an ass, and upon a colt the foal of an ass." *KJV*.

Jesus was coming, not as a triumphant ruler with a charging steed and war chariot, as most invading rulers would come. Rather, he came humbly riding on a donkey. John tells us that Jesus' disciples did not comprehend what was happening at that time. There was some recognition of Jesus' Messianic role. That he was God made flesh, the King of Kings, who was coming as the Saviour of all humankind – this was not fully grasped. It was only when he had died and had risen from the dead and the Holy Spirit had been poured out that the disciples fully understood the significance of these events.

ENTRY INTO JERUSALEM

This event of entry into Jerusalem was the beginning of Jesus' passion. It points us to his journey to the cross. Anyone who attracted a following was a threat to the governing Roman authorities. They feared uprisings, and one who was heralded as a king was dangerous. Little did they know that Jesus was a king. He was bringing to us God's kingdom.

The wise men at his birth sought the newborn king. Now the crowds heralded him as a king. Jesus entered Jerusalem in a triumphant procession. The Pharisees exclaimed that the whole world was coming after him. This was more true than they realized. His hour was coming. His death was approaching. The reason he came to earth was reaching its fulfillment and that would not be a journey upwards, but first downwards to the lowest point in human history, when he was crucified and bore the sin of the world.

Jesus used his entry into Jerusalem as an opportunity to present himself and his mission. Where Zechariah speaks of triumph and victory, the New Testament shows his entry to be humble.

The people around Jesus were crying for help: "Lord save us!" They would have been thinking of Zechariah's word about victory and triumph, hardly about humility. They were looking for a king that would bring political deliverance. Jesus was there to bring about another type of deliverance. Riding on the donkey, Jesus was pointing to God's mission and God's kingdom. He was choosing to face Jerusalem and choosing the cross. Beyond the cross was the resurrection and the open door for each one of us to enter into the presence of our heavenly Father. The victory and triumph were ahead, but not before the cross on which Jesus was to die for our sins.

The irony is that while they cried for a victorious king to save them, that is exactly what Jesus was intending to do. He would die as king of the Jews, but he would do so to save all of humankind. He was going to answer the prayer of the crowd. He was also going to fulfill the real meaning of Passover and what it meant to be released from the bondage of slavery. It might not be the slavery of Egypt, but it was the bondage of sin.

Jesus was getting ready to die for every one of us, and that includes people the world over who have lived, right through history. As King of Kings and Lord of Lords, his saving act was completely effective in saving us all from the effects and contamination of sin. We are saved from sin and saved to be God's children. That victory procession is one which we join, and we add our cries of "Hosanna, blessed is he who comes in the name of the Lord."

When we talk about what reconciliation means, we may open the dictionary and find that it has to do with resolving conflict and fractured relationships. We can understand it as about a relationship that broke down and then something happened to restore it. When Christians talk about redemption they tell a story about the love of God who sent his Son into the world. This story includes the birth of Jesus into this world and takes us to his death on the cross, his resurrection, and his ascension into heaven.

STUDY QUESTIONS

1. Why did Matthew use the genealogy or family tree of Jesus at the beginning of his gospel?
2. Why was prayer so important to Jesus?
3. What do you learn from the account in Matthew 14:13–21 when Jesus multiplied the loaves and the fishes to feed the crowd of people?
4. What is meant by the word transfiguration?
5. What is the significance of the Passover celebration?
6. Discuss the importance of Jesus' entry into Jerusalem.

Chapter 14
The Death and Resurrection of Jesus

In our consideration of the death and resurrection of Jesus, we reach the pinnacle of human history. We follow the pathway that Jesus and his disciples trod to reach this climax, which included their parting meal that came to be known as the Last Supper. According to the synoptic gospels, this was a Passover meal with rich symbolism.

THE PATHWAY TO CRUCIFIXION

Even before Jesus was arrested, as he walked with them towards Jerusalem, he began to instruct his disciples about the fact that he would soon be arrested, suffer, and die on a cross. This was not what his disciples expected. This was not the kind of final battle that they thought the Messiah would be involved in. Jesus would not be killing their enemies but rather giving up his life on a cruel Roman cross. It took them a while to understand that this was the final battle between the kingdom of God and the powers of evil. Jesus would be the victor in taking the sin of the world on himself. The shame of the cross would be turned into the victory of God over sin and death.

THE LAST SUPPER

Jesus celebrated a Passover meal with his disciples, which has traditionally become known as the Last Supper. The symbols of the meal were soon to be interpreted in a new way. Jesus stood in continuity with the saving acts of God in the past, but he was now the redeemer. The lamb would soon be slain. We are linked to the words of John the Baptist as he pointed to Jesus, 'the lamb of God' who takes away the sins of the world. Jesus was pointing to a new act of redemption which was the deliverance of humanity from sin. The prophecy of Isaiah in chapter 53:7–9 speaks of the suffering servant, who would be like a lamb that is led to the slaughter and on whom all the guilt and sin of the world are laid.

[7] "He was oppressed, and he was afflicted, yet he opened not his mouth: he is brought as a lamb to the slaughter, and as a sheep before her shearers is dumb, so he openeth not his mouth. [8] He was taken from prison and from judgment: and who shall declare his generation? for he was cut off out of the land of the living: for the transgression of my people was he stricken. [9] And he made his grave with the wicked, and with the rich in his death; because he had done no violence, neither was any deceit in his mouth." *KJV.*

The bread and wine of the Passover meal were also given a new meaning as he took the unleavened bread, gave thanks, and broke it. When he gave it to the disciples he called it his body broken for them. They were to remember him by this means. When he took the cup of wine after the supper, he called it the new covenant in his blood, which was poured out for them.

These words have shaped the Christian understanding of what Christ did for us in dying on the cross. They foreshadowed the events that were to take place, and for us, they are to be remembered and proclaimed. We remember the event, but we are also to think about what it means to us. This is a clear statement of Jesus telling us the meaning of his death. Jesus was among them as one who serves. Mark 10:44–45 tells us that the Son of Man came not to be served but to serve, and to give his life as a ransom for many.

A ransom was paid for those who were in captivity. They were held against their will, unable to break free. Unless someone came to liberate them they would remain trapped. Someone who paid the ransom price on their behalf would set them free. The greater the value of the person, the greater the ransom which the captors would demand. God showed his love for us by paying an astonishing ransom for us. While we were yet sinners, Jesus the Messiah died for us. God loves us and shows his love for us by paying the ransom price which was the death of his Son Jesus.

As Augustine shows us, we are trapped and need rescuing. We are in darkness and need the light. We are ill and need a healer. We are injured and need someone to bind up our wounds. We are captives and need to be

THE MOUNT OF OLIVES AND GETHSEMANE

The Mount of Olives was part of the route from Jerusalem to Bethany. During biblical times this mountain, which overlooks the Kidron Valley and has awe-inspiring views of the city of David, was covered in ancient olive trees. It was here that Jesus came with his disciples after the Passover meal they had shared. All except Judas Iscariot, who had slipped out to betray him.

It was here that he encouraged his disciples and gave them a final warning of his impending death. He told them that after his resurrection, he would go before them into Galilee.[1] It was at the place called Gethsemane that he knelt to pray with a heavy heart. He asked his Father that, if possible, he should take away this cup of suffering from him. Even though he was suffering from the sorrow of what was to come, he submitted to the will of his Father and gave up his own will. It was here that he was betrayed into the hands of a great multitude with swords and staves from the chief priests and scribes and elders.[2]

THE INTERROGATION

The trial before Annas and then Caiaphas, the high priest, shows contradictions between the false witnesses. Finally, the high priest asks Jesus the question, "Are you the Christ, the Son of the blessed one?" To this Jesus replies, "I am."[3] Jesus also quotes from Psalm 110 and Daniel 7 saying, "You will see the Son of Man sitting at the right hand of power, and coming in the clouds of heaven." *KJV.*

Jesus is telling Caiaphas that he will witness his vindication in the events that follow his death. This explains why Pilate came to crucify Jesus with the words 'King of the Jews' written above his head. It also helps to explain why Jesus' followers regarded him as the Messiah after his resurrection.

1. Mark 14: 27–28
2. Mark 14:43
3. Mark 14:61–62

PART FOUR: JESUS, SON OF GOD

THE PLACE OF THE SKULL

After his flogging and Pilate's sentence of death by crucifixion, Jesus stumbled under the weight of the cross to the place of his crucifixion. At nine o'clock in the morning, he was stripped naked and Roman soldiers nailed his wrists and feet to the cross, which was set between two others. Even as the soldiers drove the nails into his flesh he was asking his Father to forgive them, for they did not know what they were doing.[4] Some jeered at him, while one man next to him stated the truth that Jesus had done nothing wrong, and asked to be remembered when Jesus came into his kingdom.[5]

As he hung in extreme suffering on the cross, darkness covered the whole land from noon for three hours, until Jesus cried out in agony, "My God, my God, why have you forsaken me?"[6] Jesus was bearing the sin of the world, and he felt that he was forsaken by his Father. Then, as his life drained away, he called out a final time, "It is finished! Father, into your hands I commit my spirit."[7] *NRSV*. His work of salvation was done.

At this moment in the temple, the heavy curtain separating the holy of holies from the outer sections was rent in two from top to bottom. This was a divine action, showing that the death of Jesus had opened the way into the very presence of God. "Let us therefore come boldly unto the throne of grace, that we may obtain mercy, and find grace to help in time of need."[8] *KJV*.

USING OUR IMAGINATION

One of the writers on Christian Spirituality, Ignatius Loyola (1491–1556), stresses the importance of imagination in our encounter with the crucified Christ. Our minds must think about the Passion narratives for us to find the meaning of the cross for ourselves. We can imagine ourselves standing before the cross and joining the disciples to understand and appreciate what Jesus has done for us. He suggests a dialogue that we can have with Jesus, reflecting on what he has done, and then using this reflection for self-examination.

4. Luke 23:34
5. Luke 23:40–42
6. Mark 15:34
7. Luke 23:46
8. Hebrews 4:16

We can imagine Jesus our Lord hanging on the cross. We can talk to him about how the creator became a human being and how he submitted himself to death for our sins.

Perhaps the most important question that we can ask is why did Jesus, who lived a sinless and perfect life, have to die like a common criminal on the cross? The simple answer is that it was you and I who should have died for our sinfulness, but Jesus took our place. He died that we might be forgiven. He died so that we can be cleansed of all our sins and enter into the presence of a holy God. Jesus has taken away our sin and given us new life and the hope of living for eternity with God. We only have to turn to Jesus and ask for him to make that a reality in our lives.

Jesus, I am a sinner, but I turn to you today and thank you for taking away all my sin when you died on the cross. I want to live for you from this day, drawing on the new life that you have made available for me.

When we face dark and difficult times that feel like a dark night, it is only by faith that we can look forward to the morning of resurrection. When God seems hidden, we know that Jesus did not remain in that tomb, for he rose to new life.

THE SIGNIFICANCE OF JESUS' DEATH

Stanley Grenz gives some helpful themes about the theological significance of the death of Jesus.[9]

First, New Testament authors have seen it as an *example* to us. His conduct and attitudes, even as he faced death, can influence the way we approach life having patience in suffering, showing humility, and loving others.[10]

Second, his death is our *ransom*.[11] He has won the victory over powers that have kept us in bondage including the law of sin of death and our inability to keep God's law in our own strength.[12]

Third, his death is our *expiation*. This is the idea that human sin is covered over, protecting us from the wrath of God. Hebrews 2:17 explains that as a high priest, Jesus makes atonement for the sins of the people. The imagery of the mercy seat (Greek – *hilasterion*) in the tabernacle suggests

---

9. Grenz, *Theology*, 345–348.
10. 1 Peter 2:21–23, Philippians 2:3–8, and Ephesians 5:2.
11. Ephesians 1:7, Hebrews 9:12, and 1 Timothy 2:6.
12. Colossians 2:15, Galatians 3:13, and Romans 8:2.

that the death of Jesus covers our sin. For Jesus entered the heavenly holy of holies bearing his blood, which he poured out on the mercy seat of the ark of the covenant, forgiving our sins and restoring our relationship with God. Grenz points out that Paul writes in Romans 3:25-26 that God "put forth Christ as a *hilasterion* or mercy seat."[13] This extends the explanation from Hebrews 2:17 to express how he passes over our sins and justifies all who express faith in him. It also shows that with Christ's death being the new focus of atonement, he covers our sins and replaces the mercy seat of the tabernacle which was previously needed for the forgiveness of sins. The work of Jesus now enables God to forgive our sins and to declare that we are righteous based on what Jesus has done. Declaring us righteous also means that we now have a restored relationship with God. The practice of repeated sacrifices is no longer necessary or required as the book of Hebrews points out, because Jesus died once for all sin and made a perfect atoning sacrifice with his death on the cross.

Fourth, Jesus is our *reconciliation* and he saves us by his life. Romans 5:10-11:

¹⁰ "For if, when we were enemies, we were reconciled to God by the death of his Son, much more, being reconciled, we shall be saved by his life. ¹¹ And not only so, but we also joy in God through our Lord Jesus Christ, by whom we have now received the atonement." *KJV*.

From being enemies of God, we now have a new relationship with him and enjoy fellowship and reconciliation. This also extends to barriers between human beings being broken down and even the reconciliation of all things in heaven and on earth.[14] God's overall purpose for the atonement which Jesus achieved is worked out with the anticipation of a redeemed humankind, a renewed creation, and the enjoyment for all of creation of the life and presence of the triune God. God is establishing the eschatological community which marks his reign. Through his life and teaching, Jesus has been revealing God's plan and purpose, and the cross and resurrection are the climax of his life.

Paul was able to say that above all else he would boast in the cross of our Lord Jesus Christ.[15] Why would Paul choose to boast in the gruesome death of his Lord? He tells us in Romans 5:8 "But God commendeth his love toward us, in that, while we were yet sinners, Christ died for us." *KJV*.

---

13. Grenz, *Theology*, 347.
14. Ephesians 2:11-22 and Colossians 1:19-20.
15. Galatians 6:14

In other words, God is showing his love for us; even while we are sinners he sent his Son to die for us. The love of God is prepared to suffer for the ones that he loves. Not only does he suffer, but through the cross, righteousness from God comes to us through faith in Jesus Christ.

THE RESURRECTION OF JESUS

The women mentioned in Luke 24:1–12 were prevented from coming to the tomb of Jesus any earlier on account of the Sabbath Day, on which no work could be done. By the time Jesus had died and been taken down from the cross, the Sabbath Day preparations would have already begun, as that started on a Friday evening. Joseph of Arimathea was a secret disciple of Jesus and he asked Pilate that he might take away the body of Jesus.

John 19:39–40 tells that Nicodemus brought about a hundredweight of a mixture of myrrh and aloes and with Joseph of Arimathea they took the body of Jesus and bound it in linen cloths with the spices as it was the custom for burial among the Jews. The synoptic gospels give a slightly different rendering. Matthew 27: 59–60 speaks of Joseph taking the body and wrapping it in a clean linen cloth, and laying it in his own new tomb which he had hewn out of the rock. He rolled a great stone to the door of the tomb. Mark 15: 46 is similar. Joseph bought a linen cloth and taking Jesus down he wound him in the linen cloth and laid him in a tomb which had been hewn out of a rock and rolled a stone against the door of the tomb. Luke 23:53 also describes that Joseph took the body of Jesus down and wrapped it in a linen cloth and laid him in a tomb that was hewn in stone, where no person had been laid.

Now on the first day of the week, the women were able to come back to embalm his body with the spices which they had prepared. Luke 23:55 tells us that the women from Galilee followed Joseph and saw the tomb and how his body was laid. They must have decided that they still needed to anoint the body of Jesus with spices and rewrap his body in the linen cloth. They had probably woken while it was still dark to prepare the spices, and since it was still very early in the morning they would probably have walked to the tomb before the sun rose and while the dawn was only just beginning to lighten the sky. It was just light enough to find their way along the silent streets. They were eager to do their job, although their hearts were torn by the events of that darkest of days when their Lord and master had been cruelly tortured, beaten, and then crucified.

Part Four: Jesus, Son of God

Perhaps many thoughts were going through their minds. He had helped and healed so many, and yet this had happened to him. They had seen miracles take place as he multiplied the loaves and the fishes. How many times had they heard the disciples tell the story of the healing of the lepers and the stilling of the storm when they nearly lost their boat and their lives in the violent storm that swept down onto the Sea of Galilee?

They all loved him. He had spoken to them as no other person ever had. He had filled their lives with new hope and a new purpose. They experienced him as new life, new light, and understanding. Now all that was swept away by the events of the last few days. Hope had drained out of them but their love for Jesus drove them on to honor him one last time, by spreading the spices over his cold, dead body and wrapping his body with the linen cloths once more.

Perhaps they worried about how they would roll that heavy stone away from the entrance to the tomb. They had called on some of their women friends to come along and help them roll away the heaviest burden they had ever faced. It was more than just removing the stone. It was facing once again the torn and mangled body of their friend and reliving the horrors of his crucifixion.

When they arrived at the tomb they found the stone rolled away. At least they could go in. Perhaps they wondered why the stone was no longer sealing the tomb. When they went into the tomb it was clear that the body of Jesus was not there.

If ever you have lost something precious you will know what it feels like. I once lost my daughters on a crowded beach in Cornwall. They were old enough to wander off to play, but I panicked when I realized I could not find them among the mass of beach umbrellas and people. I felt sick and almost faint with fright. What relief when they came into sight! Did these women feel the same when they realized that Jesus was no longer in the tomb? They had time to stand and think about the options. Had his body been stolen? Had someone else come to take his body away? Was it the Romans? If only they had come earlier.

WHAT THEY FOUND IN THE TOMB

Nothing could prepare them for what happened next. The Bible says that two men with gleaming clothes that shone like lightning were there. These were not ordinary men. In the half-light of the empty tomb, they shone with a light that was so bright that the women could not look at them. Their legs gave way and they bowed right down with their faces to the ground in their fright. The men questioned them as to why they were looking for the living among the dead. They told the women that he was risen, just as he had told them. Then they remembered what Jesus had said.

The mistake these women had made is that they were looking for a dead Savior. How often do we too make that mistake? We know Jesus lived on this earth and died on the cross. Do we forget that he was raised from the dead as he promised he would? Do we live our lives in our own strength, or do we look to a living Savior who can cleanse us from all sin and strengthen us to live the life that he has planned for us?

We are not called to self-effort religion. We are not called to please God by climbing up the ladder of progress. We are called to a fresh discovery that we cling to a risen and living Savior who loves us and draws us close to himself as we turn daily to him. He has promised us an easy yoke and a light burden. That is because he is with us to lead us and guide us through life. We bow to his will for our lives and we discover that is an easy yoke.

The words of the angels that appeared to the women remind us that the events of the cross and his death did not take Jesus by surprise. He knew what lay up ahead for him. He also knew that he would be raised from the dead. He had even taught his disciples that, but they had forgotten as the events of the past few days had swept over them. Now, with the evidence of the empty tomb and the appearance of the angels, they remembered.

When the women went back to the other apostles and told them what they had seen, they did not believe them. Words of truth seemed to them like nonsense.

SEEKING THE LIVING GOD

If we think of our own lives, perhaps we too seek the living among the dead. Perhaps there are times when instead of seeking the living God, we turn to things that bring only death and dissatisfaction into our lives. Do we choose to accept the bad news that is broadcast or look to the good news of Jesus Christ? Do we believe that God is at work in the life of people, mending broken hearts and broken families? Or do we believe that our world is only filled with the bad news that comes from the media? Do we believe that we can bring our difficulties and our neighbors' troubles to God? Or do we think that we must struggle with life on our own?

Peter got up and ran to the tomb. He saw the strips of linen lying in a heap, and then he went away, wondering to himself what had happened. We need to be like Peter and see for ourselves that the tomb is empty. We don't have to go away wondering what has happened. We know that Jesus has risen and that he lives. That makes all the difference to our lives because we know that we worship and serve a living God. We have hope because we know that the Scriptures are true. Jesus is at work in our lives by his Holy Spirit. We look forward to the fact that when we die, that is not the end. The hope of the resurrection is for us too.

JESUS APPEARS TO HIS DISCIPLES

John 20:19-23: [19] On the evening of that day, the first day of the week, the doors being locked where the disciples were for fear of the Jews, Jesus came and stood among them and said to them, "Peace be with you." [20] When he had said this, he showed them his hands and his side. Then the disciples were glad when they saw the Lord. [21] Jesus said to them again, "Peace be with you. As the Father has sent me, even so I am sending you." [22] And when he had said this, he breathed on them and said to them, "Receive the Holy Spirit. [23] If you forgive the sins of any, they are forgiven them; if you withhold forgiveness from any, it is withheld." *ESV.*

The account in this reading takes place after the resurrection of Jesus, but the doors of the house where the disciples are gathered are locked. Fear has gripped the hearts of the disciples as they are anxious about whether they too will suffer the tragic fate of Jesus. Understandably, they worry that the temple authorities will find and arrest them.

Instead, Jesus wastes no time after his resurrection in coming to them and standing in their midst. No doubt this is a miraculous appearance since John has told us that the doors were firmly locked. Just how Jesus appeared among them we cannot speculate on. His words 'peace be with you' was a standard Hebrew greeting of *'shalom.'* This is still used in Israel today to say hello. Shalom is more than a greeting. It has the meaning of wishing good health and well-being.

Jesus is also summing up his work and presence in the world as one who brings peace on so many levels. Peace is a gift of his kingdom. Earlier in John's gospel, Jesus promised that this peace would be his gift to them. Now he brings it with his presence coming into this anxious gathering.

What is the disciples' response to him? Even this has been told earlier in John's gospel when Jesus had told them that they would weep and mourn while the world rejoices, but their grief would turn to joy when they saw him again and that no one would take away their joy. As they see the risen Lord Jesus in the room, the disciples are filled with joy.

Why had Jesus come to his disciples, apart from showing them that he has indeed risen? One of his final tasks was to commission his followers, as he was commissioned by his Father. Just as Jesus was God's special agent in the world, so too his disciples were to become his agents. They would soon be going to work in the world and bring the love of God to many communities. They would witness to the reality of the risen Lord Jesus Christ. They would bear the truth of Jesus' words to many people.

THOMAS THE UNBELIEVING DISCIPLE

There was one disciple who was not with the others when Jesus came. Perhaps Thomas was trying to cope with the events of the past few days in his own way, by going off to be alone. When the others saw him and told him that they had seen the Lord, Thomas replied: "Except I shall see in his hands the print of the nails, and put my finger into the print of the nails, and thrust my hand into his side, I will not believe."[16] *KJV*. Does Thomas speak for many who say, 'Give me proof, and I'll believe.'

God gave Thomas time to think about the situation. Jesus came back to the disciples a week later, and this time Thomas was with them. The doors were still locked. Jesus came with the same greeting, 'Peace be with you.' He turned right round to Thomas and told him to put his finger into his side and to see his hands. He admonished Thomas, telling him to see and believe.

Thomas may have been slow to believe, but now he grasped the implication of the resurrection and said: 'My Lord and my God.' The evidence was clear and Thomas's faith now rested on solid rock.

Perhaps this story is given for us, that we too can believe that Jesus rose again and appeared to his disciples. We too are given the gift of the Holy Spirit. When we receive Jesus Christ as our Saviour and Lord and enter into his kingdom, we are filled with the Holy Spirit.

16. John 20:25

We are also called to be those who witness to the risen Lord Jesus and tell others of our faith in him. Our belief in the resurrection of Jesus Christ is necessary if we are going to follow Jesus.

STUDY QUESTIONS

1. How did Jesus interpret the last Passover meal that he ate with his disciples?
2. What was the significance of the death of Jesus?
3. How did the empty tomb impact the women who came to embalm the body of Jesus?
4. What can we learn from the disciple Thomas?

Chapter 15

Commissioned for Mission

As we read the gospels, we see the ways Jesus is preparing his disciples for their future ministry as he travels with them and teaches them what it means to live in the kingdom of God. The disciples are commissioned during the life of Jesus and also after his resurrection. We read of Jesus choosing his disciples and preparing them for the task of reaching out with his message.

THE OUTPOURING OF THE HOLY SPIRIT

John 7:37–39 tells of the living water which will impact the lives of his followers when the Holy Spirit is poured out later. [37] "In the last day, that great day of the feast, Jesus stood and cried, saying, If any man thirst, let him come unto me, and drink. [38] He that believeth on me, as the scripture hath said, out of his belly shall flow rivers of living water. [39] (But this spake he of the Spirit, which they that believe on him should receive: for the Holy Ghost was not yet given; because that Jesus was not yet glorified.)" *KJV*.

JESUS COMMISSIONS HIS DISCIPLES

When he was raised from the dead, Jesus commissioned his disciples to make all nations into his followers. Matthew 28:18–20:

[18] "And Jesus came and spake unto them, saying, All power is given unto me in heaven and in earth. [19] Go ye therefore, and teach all nations, baptizing them in the name of the Father, and of the Son, and of the Holy

Ghost: [20] Teaching them to observe all things whatsoever I have commanded you: and, lo, I am with you always, even unto the end of the world." *KJV.*

Thus those who have responded to his call are sent out to continue the mission and to establish the kingdom of God on the earth through the proclamation of the Good News.

One important part of Jesus' commission is his empowering. At Jesus' baptism, God had sent down the Holy Spirit to enable him for his ministry. Jesus' baptism was not only the water that he went down into but even more important was the anointing of the Holy Spirit as he came up out of the water.

John the Baptist had already prophesied, "I baptize you with water for repentance. But after me comes one who is more powerful than I, whose sandals I am not worthy to carry. He will baptize you with the Holy Spirit and with fire." [1]*NIV.* The Spirit is the source of eternal life and God's spiritual refreshment and renewal that is offered to his disciples. They will be sent out and be empowered by the Holy Spirit, just as Jesus had been.

The Holy Spirit who had been at work in Jesus' public ministry is now given to the disciples in a personal way. Jesus breathes on them and says, "Receive the Holy Spirit."

This echoes the words of Jesus at the Feast of Tabernacles when he offered the living water. We also hear Jesus offering this living water to the Samaritan woman at the well.

This refers to the Holy Spirit, who could not be given until Jesus had been glorified. Now the hour of glorification was at hand. Jesus had just died and been raised from the dead. He would soon be departing back to heaven. He would pour out the Holy Spirit into his disciples' lives.

Jesus' breathing on them recounts Genesis [27] when God made Adam and breathed into him the breath of life. Here Jesus is recreating anew what sin had ruined in the Garden of Eden.

FOUR PORTRAITS OF JESUS' MISSION

In the visions of Ezekiel and of John, the author of the book of Revelation, we read of the four faces of the cherubim and the four living creatures around the throne of God.[2]

1. Matthew 3:11
2. Ezekiel 1:4–28 and Revelation 4–6

Irenaeus described them as 'images of the disposition of the Son of God', the aspects of his purpose or mission — the lion and his royal power, the ox and his sacrifice, the human and his incarnation, and the eagle and his Spirit.[3]

The four symbols of the man, the lion, the ox, and the eagle have long been thought to refer to the gospel evangelists Matthew, Mark, Luke, and John. Richard Burridge has suggested how each of them has developed these symbols in their account of Jesus' mission, reflecting in different ways his calling and how this can help us to understand our callings to mission and to respond to the commission of Jesus.

JESUS AS TEACHER

Matthew's gospel gives us an insight into Jesus as a teacher. In chapter 5 we are told he went up the mountain and when he sat down, his disciples came to him and he taught them. The Sermon on the Mount follows, which astounds the crowd for the authority which Jesus displays. There are also another four sermons in Matthew's gospel. Burridge suggests that there are similarities between Jesus and Moses in Matthew's gospel, including the mention of Jesus going up to a high mountain both to teach, to pray, to heal, to feed the five thousand, the scene of the transfiguration, and the final commissioning of the disciples.[4]

Teaching others about the kingdom of God and all that Jesus taught them was the main focus of Jesus' commission to his disciples. For some, this may be preaching sermons, while for others it may be by encounters with individuals or small groups. Just as Jesus lived his life among them and his life matched up to his teaching, so our lives must match up to our words, which are drawn out of our life experience.

Romans 12:6–7 is one of the Pauline passages which tells of gifts of grace (charismata), including the exercise of teaching, that is often linked to pastoral gifts. Ephesians 4:7–16 also mentions the gifts given to equip the saints for the work of ministry and the perfecting of the body of Christ. These are given for the benefit of the whole body of Christ so that it is built up and can grow and flourish and reach out to others in society. Teaching will require time for studying the Bible and prayer. For all of us, being a lifelong learner is necessary for us to understand our faith and how we can

---

3. Burridge, *Four Ministries*, 6.
4. Burridge, *Four Ministries*, 19.

share it with others. 2 Timothy 2:2: "and what you have heard from me through many witnesses entrust to faithful people who will be able to teach others as well." *NRSV.*

2 Timothy 2:15: "Do your best to present yourself to God as one approved, a worker who has no need to be ashamed, rightly handling the word of truth." *ESV*

For the disciples to be able to fulfill their calling to teach, they first need to establish a sound theological basis that will enable them to handle the Scriptures and be able to interpret them correctly, to make them understandable to others.

CARING FOR THE POOR AND MARGINALIZED

Luke's gospel is depicted by the hard-working ox, which drags heavy burdens and is also a sacrificial animal. Luke shows Jesus meeting with different kinds of people as he spreads the good news and heals them. Women, children, lepers, the crippled, blind people, and tax collectors are among those who find a place in Luke's gospel. Both women and men appear in Jesus's parables, and women were among his disciples, including Joanna, Susanna, Mary, and Martha. The marginalized come into his teaching and ministry, such as the Good Samaritan and the Roman centurion, and mention is made of women who came to watch as he made his way to be crucified.

Fulfilling the great commission is going to include caring for others and helping to meet their needs. Jesus sent out the twelve disciples to preach the kingdom of God and to heal the sick.[5] He later sent out seventy-two in pairs to prepare the way for his coming.[6] When doing a three-year exploration on Missional Church, we used Luke 10:1–17 every time we met for a whole year, in a process called dwelling in the Word. Partnership for Missional Church is a course developed by Pat Kiefert and is used by many churches to develop their missional outreach. Repeating the study of the same Scriptural passage over some time shows you how rich the Word of God is and how much you can glean from a seemingly well-known passage.

We see that Jesus tells his disciples the harvest is great, but the laborers are few. They are to pray that the Lord of the harvest will send out laborers into the harvest field. Not only are we to go out but we are to pray that God

---

5. Luke 6:12–16 and 9:1–6
6. Luke 10:1–17

will send us and others to share the good news of Jesus Christ. This will include seeking those who are weak, sick, lonely, and powerless in society and often forgotten by others. To have the strength and wisdom needed for this caring and sharing ministry, we need to pray that the Holy Spirit will enable us to share with others the compassion of Jesus and our testimony of what God has done in our own lives. Luke wrote the book of Acts, which includes many examples of the empowering of the Holy Spirit for the work of ministry and outreach.

STRUGGLE AND SUFFERING

The gospel of Mark highlights the struggles that Jesus faced in his ministry. They came from his family who misunderstood him, from the religious authorities who persecuted him, and from the struggle between good and evil, the Holy Spirit of God and Satan. We read that when the Holy Spirit drove Jesus out into the wilderness after his baptism, he was alone with wild beasts and he faced temptation from what Mark calls 'the satan.' Jesus had to face his accuser just as we face opposition in ministry.[7]

As Jesus returned to start his ministry by calling his disciples, they began to see Jesus' struggle with the forces of evil as he drove out unclean spirits and healed people of illnesses.

His disciples, when asked, "But whom say ye that I am?"[8] *KJV*, were able, through Peter, to answer correctly "Thou art the Christ." Yet when Jesus told them of his forthcoming death at the hands of the religious authorities, Peter began to rebuke him, for he did not understand the plan of God for Jesus. Jesus, in turn, rebuked Peter and told them what a follower of his can expect: "Whosoever will come after me, let him deny himself, and take up his cross, and follow me."[9] *KJV*.

Jesus' final battle against evil is played out on the cross as he cries out, "My God, my God, why hast thou forsaken me?"[10] *KJV*.

Following the way of the cross will mean different things for different people. It may include rejection and misunderstanding from family, friends, or society. This is particularly true in those situations where there is open hostility to Christianity. For some, it may mean suffering and death.

---

7. Burridge, *Four Ministries*, 107.
8. Mark 8:29
9. Mark 8:34
10. Mark 15:34

For every Christian, there is a cost to following Jesus. To enable us to keep following will require times of quiet and prayer, to maintain our relationship with God.

ABIDE IN ME

John's gospel shows Jesus' divine power and miracles which he calls 'signs.' These include turning water into wine at the wedding at Cana in Galilee, which reveals his glory.[11] Other signs include the healing of the son of an official, a paralytic healed, a man born blind receiving his sight, the miracle of the multiplication of the loaves and fishes, Jesus walking on water, and raising Lazarus from the dead, when Jesus proclaimed 'I am the resurrection and the life.'[12]

Just as the signs pointed to Jesus, and his disciples believed in him, so we too are like signposts that point to him. Jesus' farewell to his disciples encouraged them to abide in his love as the fruit on the vine must abide or remain on the vine.[13] Abiding in Jesus and the Father through the Holy Spirit is vitally important. The Holy Spirit is alongside us to teach and guide us into all truth and also to comfort us. Paul tells us to be continually filled with the Holy Spirit.[14] This can be a daily prayer for us, as we carry out the commission that Jesus has given us to build up the church.

THE SECOND COMING OF JESUS CHRIST

"But in those days, after that suffering, the sun will be darkened, and the moon will not give its light, and the stars will be falling from heaven, and the powers in the heavens will be shaken."[15] *NRSV.*

Mark 13 invites us to watch and wait for the return of Christ in his glory. This will be a season of God's hope and grace in a time of conflict. We will learn to listen and to pay attention to what is happening around us and in us. We are called to beware and keep alert, for we do not know when the time will come.

11. John 2:1–14
12. John 11:1–44
13. John 15:1–11
14. Ephesians 5:18
15. Mark 13:24–25

Jesus is describing to his disciples what the occasion of his coming again will be like. It will be a time of distress. Then the Son of Man will come in the clouds with great power and glory. Jesus will come again in a time of cosmological confusion. Mark 13:26-27:

[26] "Then they will see 'the Son of Man coming in clouds' with great power and glory. [27] Then he will send out the angels, and gather his elect from the four winds, from the ends of the earth to the ends of heaven." NRSV.

The dominion of Jesus is everlasting and will not pass away. His kingdom is one that will never be destroyed. Charles Wesley wrote a hymn that describes this time when the angels will gather in Jesus' followers, from every nook and cranny of this world.

> Lo, he comes with clouds descending
> Once for favoured sinners slain;
> Thousand thousand saints attending
> Swell the triumph of his train:
> Alleluia! Alleluia!
> God appears on earth to reign.[16]

When it comes to God's timetable for the end we cannot know. We have to get on with living faithfully and be who God called us to be, a people of love and grace and open to the working of the Holy Spirit in our lives. We should not be obsessed with trying to work out when Christ will return. When he lived on the earth not even Jesus knew when he would return again, neither did the angels, but only the Father knew.

We are to be alert to what God is doing in the world and watch for the signs of God's kingdom and be involved in it.

Jesus came up with the declaration in Mark 13:31 "Heaven and earth will pass away, but my words will not pass away."

History has proved him correct to the smallest details. We can trust all that he said. We can also trust that he will return, and we need to be on guard and alert. Jesus compares his coming to a man who goes away and leaves his home in the charge of his servants, who each have an assigned task. We must be like the man at the door who keeps watch. Life will not go on forever. All of life is moving towards Jesus Christ, described in Colossians 1:15-16:

---

16. Hymnary.org/text/lo he comes with clouds descending…

[15] "Who is the image of the invisible God, the firstborn of every creature: [16] For by him were all things created, that are in heaven, and that are in earth, visible and invisible, whether they be thrones, or dominions, or principalities, or powers: all things were created by him, and for him:" *KJV*.

There is a growing consensus in New Testament theology that "the Kingdom of God is in some sense present and future."[17] Rudolf Otto in this book *The Kingdom of God and the Son of Man* explains that the Kingdom of God is the heavenly realm where God's will is done and where God rules.

> The heavenly realm is a "wholly other" existence, and Jesus announced the coming of this miraculous supernatural realm. This event is exclusively God's deed and will mean the breaking off of history and the descent of the heavenly realm to earth. The Kingdom of heaven will come down from above and effect a marvelous transformation of the world. The Lord's Prayer is a petition for the coming of this supernatural, heavenly realm. However, Jesus believed that the Kingdom was already in process of coming.[18]

We are encouraged to look up. The grace of God teaches us to say, "No," to ungodliness and to live self-controlled and upright lives in this present age, while we wait for the blessed hope – the glorious appearing of our Lord and Saviour Jesus Christ.

We need to say the age-old declaration of '*Hineni*' – 'here am I, Lord' that began with Abraham, was repeated by Moses, by Samuel as a child, and affirmed by the prophet Isaiah when confronted by the awesome holiness of God. It continued with Mary and the early disciples, and above all, it was demonstrated in the willingness of Jesus to fulfill the call of God upon his life. This is a response to the call of God in our lives too.

STUDY QUESTIONS

1. How did Jesus commission his disciples and what can we learn from this about our calling to mission?
2. How does Matthew's gospel help us to understand Jesus as a teacher?
3. How does Luke's gospel depict Jesus?
4. What does Mark's gospel highlight about Jesus?

---

17. Ladd, *Presence of the Future*, 3.
18. Ladd, *Presence of the Future*, 25.

5. What do you understand about abiding in Jesus from John's gospel?
6. What are we encouraged to do as we await the second coming of Jesus Christ?

Chapter 16

Conclusion

IN THIS BOOK, I have attempted to answer the question 'what is Christian theology' and given some pointers as to how we attempt to do that. Having taken the route of a brief overview of theology in history I am well aware that the ground I have covered falls short of all there is to know about this vast topic. Equally, approaching the question of the doctrine and attributes of God is not all there is to explore in the field of Christian theology. God is bigger and wiser than anything we know and also more wonderful and beautiful than anything we can imagine. Nevertheless, he still wants us to continue with the journey of getting to know him, and he takes the first steps towards us as we stumble towards knowing him. Several times I have pointed out that this discovery of God cannot be confined to our minds but needs to be lived out in the decisions and actions of our lives.

The parable comparing the house built on the rock and the house built on the sand in Matthew 7:24–27 is an apt description of how important it is that learning about God is not just hearing his word but needs to be ingrained into our lives and become the driving force in all we do and the choices we make. Otherwise, we may find our house falling flat when the testing storms of life arise.

[24] "Everyone then who hears these words of mine and does them will be like a wise man who built his house on the rock. [25] And the rain fell, and the floods came, and the winds blew and beat on that house, but it did not fall, because it had been founded on the rock. [26] And everyone who hears these words of mine and does not do them will be like a foolish man who built his house on the sand. [27] And the rain fell, and the floods came, and

Conclusion

the winds blew and beat against that house, and it fell, and great was the fall of it." *ESV.*

I hope that you, the reader, will take up the challenge to explore even further from the extensive bibliography that I have provided at the end of the book.

At the beginning of the book, I used the analogy of diving into the sea to explore what can be seen beneath the water. Use your imagination to realize that there is a vast uncharted world under there that is yet to be explored. I also used the analogy of theology being like a 'landscape of faith.' Standing on the top of a mountain in a wilderness area will afford you many aspects of God's created world that are difficult to describe to a friend. You may provide them with a sketch map but that will not be the same as actually seeing that landscape.

In your exploration, I encourage you to read some of the texts written by theologians that I have introduced in this book and find others that I have not mentioned.

I have pointed us back to the gospels and a look at the life and ministry of Jesus as well as his death, resurrection, and the commissioning of his disciples before his ascension back to heaven. Much has been written about these subjects in the field of Christology and soteriology.

I am concerned that we do not just read the Bible and works of theology and think that our task is done. This is the reason why I have included a chapter on our commissioning and our calling. We are not being offered an armchair Christianity. We are sent out like the early followers of Jesus to share our knowledge of God and his Son Jesus with the empowering of the Holy Spirit. Paul wrote in 2 Corinthians 5:20:

[20] " Therefore, we are ambassadors for Christ, God making his appeal through us. We implore you on behalf of Christ, be reconciled to God."

Many people in our world do not know God. No matter who we are and what our gifts and talents are we are created uniquely by God and empowered by his Holy Spirit to be his hands and feet in this world. How else can the love of God be communicated to those who have never heard?

> Christ has no body now but yours. Yours are the eyes through which he looks compassion on this world. Yours are the feet with which he walks to do good. Yours are the hands through which he blesses all the world. Yours are the hands, yours are the feet, yours

Part Four: Jesus, Son of God

are the eyes, you are his body. Christ has no body now on earth but yours.[1]

Most of all I hope you will turn afresh to the Scriptures that I have included and spend time thinking about them. These will help to lay a foundation of faith in your life. The grace of God has been given to us to be skilled builders that lay a foundation that is Jesus Christ and to build on it alongside others so that the church of Jesus Christ is strengthened and extended into the world.

---

1. Attributed to St Theresa of Avila.

Appendix

of Theologians Cited in This Book

William J. **Abraham**, (b. 1947) is a Northern Irish Methodist pastor and theologian. He has lived in the United States and is Professor of Wesley Studies at Southern Methodist University.

Jeff **Astley** is Professor of Religious and Spiritual Experience at Bishop Grosseteste University in Lincoln and Honorary Professor in Theology and Religion at St Chad's College, Durham University, and Visiting Professor at York St John University. He is the author or editor of over forty publications.

Augustine of Hippo, (354-430 C.E.) was a philosopher, theologian, and bishop of Hippo Regius in North Africa. He was influential in the development of Western philosophy and Christianity. He was one of the most important of the Church Fathers during the Patristic period and wrote many important works.

Karl **Barth**, (1886–1968) was a Swiss Reformed theologian and probably one of the most influential theologians in the twentieth century.

Craig **Bartholomew**, (b. 1961) was educated in South Africa and Bristol University and is a writer and the Director of Kirby Laing Institute for Christian Ethics.

Appendix

Richard **Bauckham**, is a biblical scholar, author, and theologian. He was Professor of New Testament studies at St Andrews, Scotland until 2007, and has moved to Cambridge, UK, to concentrate on research and writing.

Henry S. **Bettenson**, (1908–1979) was an English scholar, translator, and author.

John **Blanchard**, has preached and taught internationally. He is a Christian apologist and has written many books on evangelism.

Donald G. **Bloesch**, (1928–2010) was an American, progressive evangelical, and ecumenical orthodox theologian and author. He published scholarly but accessible works within the area of mainstream modern Protestant theological thinking.

Kent **Brower** is a senior Research Fellow and lecturer in Biblical Studies at the Nazarene Theological College, Manchester, UK. He has researched aspects of New Testament theology including eschatology and holiness in the Gospels.

Walter **Brueggemann**, (b. 1933) is an American Protestant Old Testament theologian, author, and scholar. He has been influential in the modern progressive Christianity movement. He was ordained in the United Church of Christ. He lectured at Eden Theological Seminary and Colombia Theological Seminary.

Richard A. **Burridge**, (b.1955) is an Anglican priest, a Biblical scholar, and was Dean of King's College, London.

Graham **Buxton** is an ordained Anglican priest with teaching experience in Australia and the United Kingdom in ministry, theology, and culture. He has taught in practical theology, pastoral ministry, science and theology. He is a professor at Fuller Theological Seminary in California, USA.

Henry **Chadwick**, (1920–2008) was an Anglican priest, academic, and theologian. He was a leading historian of the early church and was Professor at both Oxford and Cambridge, UK.

Appendix

Ivor J. **Davidson** is a British theologian and academic administrator. He has lectured in systematic and historical theology in New Zealand, the University of St Andrews, and the University of Aberdeen.

J. Scott **Duvall** is a Professor of New Testament at Ouachita Baptist University in Arkansas.

Norman **Geisler**, (1932–2019) was an American Christian theologian, writer, and philosopher. He made scholarly contributions in many fields of Christian theology and Christian apologetics.

Michael **Goheen** is Director of Theological Education of Missional Training Center and a residential scholar at Surge Network of Churches in Phoenix. He is a Professor of missional theology at Covenant Theological Seminary in St Louis.

John **Calvin**, (1509–1564) was a French theologian, pastor, and reformer during the Protestant Reformation. He lived in Geneva and developed the ideas of Christian theology which came to be called Calvinism.

Marva J. **Dawn**, (b.1948) is an American Lutheran Christian theologian, author, musician, and educator. She is a Teaching Fellow in Spiritual Theology at Regent College, Vancouver.

Gabriel **Fackre**, (1926–2018) was an American theologian and Christian minister. He wrote prolifically in the fields of theology, ethics, and mission.

David F. **Ford**, (b. 1948) is Professor of Divinity at the University of Cambridge, UK.

William H. C. **Frend**, (1916–2005) was an author, educationalist, historian, archaeologist, and priest. He was a scholar of the early Christian church.

Stanley **Grenz** is a leading evangelical theologian based at Carey Theological College in Vancouver, Canada. He has lectured throughout the world and written books on theology and postmodernism.

Appendix

Colin E. **Gunton**, (1941–2003) was Professor of Christian doctrine at King's College, London. He was a minister in the United Reform Church in the United Kingdom.

Victor P. **Hamilton**, (b. 1941) is a Canadian/American theologian. He worked at Asbury University as a Professor of theology and Old Testament and is currently professor emeritus of Old Testament.

Daniel J. **Hays** is Professor of Biblical Studies at Pruet School of Christian Studies, Ouachita Baptist University, Arkansas.

Mary **Hayter**. Author of a book about the use and abuse of the Bible in the debate about women.

Irenaeus. (c. 130–c. 202 CE) He was a Greek bishop in the south of France. He developed Christian theology by defining orthodoxy and by writing and teaching against heresy.

Veli-Matti **Kärkkäinen**, (b. 1958) is a Finnish theologian. He is a Professor of Systematic Theology at Fuller Theological Seminary in Pasadena, California and is an ordained Lutheran minister.

George E. **Ladd**, (1911–1982) was a Baptist minister and professor of New Testament and theology at Fuller Theological Seminary in Pasadena, California.

Michael **Lodahl** is a writer and professor at the Point Loma Nazarene University of Theology and World Religions in California.

Martin **Luther**, (1483–1546) was a German professor of theology, a priest, author, composer, and Augustinian monk. He was an important figure in the Reformation and rejected some of the teachings of the Roman Catholic Church.

Joseph **Mangina** is a professor of systematic theology at Wycliffe College, University of Toronto. He has authored two books on Karl Barth.

Appendix

Justin **Martyr** was born c. 100 in Samaria. He was an early Christian apologist. He was martyred for his faith. Of his work, only two apologies and a dialogue survive.

Chris **Maunder** is a senior lecturer in theology and religious studies at York St John University, North Yorkshire, England.

Mark A. **McIntosh**, (b. 1960) is an American Episcopal priest and theologian. He is a Professor of Christian Spirituality at Loyola University, Chicago.

Sally **McFague,** (1933–2019) was an American feminist Christian theologian. She was Theologian in Residence at Vancouver School of Theology, British Columbia, Canada.

Alister E. **McGrath**, (b. 1953) is an Anglican priest, theologian, author, historian, scientist, and Christian apologist. He is a professor of theology and religion at the University of Oxford, UK.

John A. **McGuckin**, (b. 1952) is an Orthodox Christian priest, theologian, church historian, and poet.

Roni **Mechanic** (b. 1948) is an ordained minister, theological educator, writer, conference speaker, and Messianic Jew.

Jürgen **Moltmann**, (born 1926) is a German Reformed theologian. He is known for his books such as *The Crucified God* and *God in Creation*.

Leon **Morris**, (1914–2006) was an Australian New Testament scholar and writer and an ordained Anglican minister.

J. E. Lesslie **Newbigin**, (1909–1998) was a British theologian, missiologist, and author. He was a bishop in the Church of South India.

Gregory of **Nyssa**, (c. 335–c. 395) was bishop of Nyssa. Gregory of Nyssa, his brother Basil of Caesarea, and Gregory of Nazianzus were known as the Cappadocian Fathers. He was a theologian who contributed to the doctrine of the Trinity and the Nicene Creed.

Appendix

Mercy A. **Oduyoye**, (b. 1934) is a Ghanaian Methodist theologian and known for her work on the theology of African women. She is the director of the Institute of African Women in Religion and Culture at Trinity Theological Seminary in Ghana.

Roger **Olson**, (b. 1952) is Professor of Christian theology and ethics at Baylor University in Waco, Texas. He is an American Baptist theologian and writer.

Origen (c.184–c.253) was an early Christian theologian and scholar from Alexandria. He wrote extensively on biblical exegesis, hermeneutics, homiletics, and spirituality. He is known as the greatest genius of the early church.

Rudolf **Otto**, (1869–1937) was a German Lutheran philosopher and comparative religionist. He was an influential scholar of religion in the early twentieth century.

James I. **Packer**, (1926–2020) was born in England and lectured at Trinity College, Bristol before moving to Canada to become one of the most influential Anglican evangelical theologians and writers in North America.

Wolfhart **Pannenberg**, (1928–2014) was a German Lutheran theologian. He was a lecturer and author of books on theology.

Arthur G. **Patzia** is a Professor of New Testament at Fuller Theological Seminary in Northern California. He has written Commentaries for the New International Bible Commentary series.

Tertullian, (c. 155–c. 240) was an early Latin Christian writer from Carthage in the Roman province of Africa.

Thomas **Torrance**, (1913–2007) was a Scottish Protestant minister and theologian of Christian dogmatics at New College, Edinburgh. He was well known for his work in the study of science and theology, and his work in systematic theology.

Williston **Walker**, (1860–1922) was an American church historian. He lectured at Hartford Seminary and Yale University.

Appendix

Keith **Ward**, (b. 1938) is a Church of England priest, philosopher, and theologian. He was Regius Professor of Divinity at Oxford University, UK and his main topics of interest were comparative theology and the relationship between science and religion.

Gordon J. **Wenham** is a lecturer in Old Testament at Trinity College, Bristol. He is a British Old Testament scholar and writer.

Christopher J. H. **Wright**, (b. 1947) is an Anglican clergyman, missiologist, and Old Testament scholar. He is the International Ministries Director of the Langham Partnership which provides scholarships and preaching training for pastors in the Majority World countries.

N. T. **Wright**, (b. 1948) is an English Anglican bishop and New Testament theologian and writer. He is a senior research fellow at Wycliffe Hall, University of Oxford, UK.

About the Author

Elisheva Mechanic was educated in South Africa and studied education at Cape Town University and through the London Montessori Training College.

She has taught in schools in South Africa and the United Kingdom. She and her husband Roni Mechanic ministered together in Cape Town, where they pioneered the first Messianic Jewish Congregation in South Africa, called Beit Ariel. They lived and studied in Israel for three years in the 1990s, together with their three children.

Beginning in 2002 Elisheva studied a Theology and Pastoral Studies Degree at the Nazarene Theological College, Manchester University, UK. In 2008–2010 Elisheva did her Ordination training and MA at Ridley College, Cambridge. Through the Cambridge Federation and Anglia Ruskin University, she was awarded her Master's Degree in Practical Theology.

Elisheva has been involved in full-time ordained ministry in the Anglican Church and has taught Cross-Cultural ministry, Biblical Studies, and theology at Bible Colleges in South Africa and Pakistan. She has ministered in South Africa, Israel, Ghana, Australia, the United States, and the United Kingdom, where she and her husband are currently living.

Bibliography

Abraham, William, J. *The Divine Inspiration of Holy Scripture*. Oxford: Oxford University Press, 1981.
The Archbishop's Council. *Common Worship: Daily Prayer*. London: Church House, 2015.
The Archbishop's Council. *Common Worship: Services and Prayers for the Church of England*. London: Church House, 2000.
Arthur, Leena A., ed. *The Prophets Speak from the Holy Scriptures*. Swindon: MediaServe, 2009.
Astley, Jeff. *Ordinary Theology: Looking, Listening and Learning in Theology*. Aldershot, Hampshire: Ashgate, 2002.
Athanasius. *The Complete Works of Saint Athanasius*. Kindle Edition. Toronto, Canada, 2016.
Augustine of Hippo. *On the Trinity*. Translated by Arthur W. Haddan. Kindle Edition. Veritatis Splendor, 2012.
Avis, Paul, ed. *Divine Revelation*. London: Dartman, Longman and Todd, 1997.
Barth, Karl. *Church Dogmatics*. London: T&T Clark, 2009.
———. *The Epistle to the Romans*. Translated by Edwyn C. Hoskyns. London: Oxford University Press, 1953.
Bartholomew, Craig, and Michael Goheen. *The Drama of Scripture: Finding our Place in the Biblical Story*. London: SPCK, 2006.
Bartholomew, Craig et al., eds. *Out of Egypt: Biblical Theology and Biblical Interpretation*. Volume 5. Grand Rapids: Zondervan, 2004.
Bauckham, Richard. *Bible and Ecology: Rediscovering the Community of Creation*. London: Darton, Longman & Todd, 2010.
Bauckham, Richard and Benjamin Drewery. *Scripture, Tradition and Reason*. Edinburgh: T&T Clark, 1988.
Bettenson, Henry and Chris Maunder. *Documents of the Christian Church*. Oxford: Oxford University Press, 1999.
Blanchard, John. *Does God believe in Atheists?* Darlington: Evangelical, 2000.
Bloesch, Donald G. *God the Almighty: Power, Wisdom, Holiness, Love*. Downers Grove, Illinois: InterVarsity, 1995.
Brower, Kent. *Holiness in the Gospels*. Kansas City, Missouri: Beacon Hill, 2005.
Brueggemann, Walter. *The Book That Breathes New Life: Scriptural Authority and Biblical Theology*. Minneapolis: Fortress, 2005.
———. *Old Testament Theology: An Introduction*. Nashville: Abingdon, 2008.
———. *Theology of the Old Testament: Testimony, Dispute, Advocacy*. Minneapolis: Fortress, 1998.

Bibliography

Burridge, Richard A. *Four Ministries One Jesus: Exploring your Vocation with the Four Gospels*. London: SPCK, 2017.
Buxton, Graham. *The Trinity, Creation, and Pastoral Ministry: Imaging the Perichoretic God*. Milton Keynes: Paternoster, 2005.
Calvin, John. *The Institutes of the Christian Religion*. Translated by Henry Beveridge, 1845. Kindle Edition, 2010.
Chadwick, Henry. *The Early Church*. England: Penguin, 1967.
Davidson, Ivor J. *The Birth of the Church: From Jesus to Constantine AD 30-312*. Volume One. Oxford: Monarch, 2005.
Dawn, Marva J. *A Royal "Waste" of Time: The Splendor of Worshiping God and Being Church for the World*. Grand Rapids: Eerdmans, 1999.
Duvall, J. Scott and J. Daniel Hays. *God's Relational Presence: The Cohesive Center of Biblical Theology*. Grand Rapids: Baker Academic, 2019.
Fackre, Gabriel. *The Christian Story*. Grand Rapids: Eerdmans, 1984.
———. *The Doctrine of Revelation. A Narrative Interpretation*. Edinburgh: Edinburgh University Press, 1997.
Ford, David. *The Modern Theologians: An Introduction to Christian Theology in the Twentieth Century*. Oxford: Blackwell, 1997.
———. *Theology: A Very Short Introduction*. Oxford: Oxford University Press, 1999.
Frend, William H.C. *The Early Church: from the Beginnings to 461*. London: SCM, 1998.
Geisler, Norman. *Christian Apologetics*. Grand Rapids: Baker Book House, 1976.
Grenz, Stanley. *Theology for the Community of God*. Grand Rapids: Eerdmans, 1994.
Grenz, Stanley and R. Olson. *Who Needs Theology? An Invitation to the Study of God*. Leicester: InterVarsity, 1996.
Gunton, Colin E. *A Brief Theology of Revelation*. London: T&T Clark, 1995.
———, ed. *The Cambridge Companion to Christian Doctrine*. Cambridge: Cambridge University Press, 1997.
———. *Theology through the Theologians: Selected Essays, 1972-1995*. London: T&T Clark, 1996.
Gunton, Colin, et al., eds. *The Practice of Theology: A Reader*. London: SCM, 2001.
Hamilton, Victor P. *The Book of Genesis Chapters 1-17*. The New International Commentary on the Old Testament. Grand Rapids: Eerdmans, 1990.
Hayter, Mary. *New Eve in Christ*. London: SPCK, 1987.
Hodgson, Peter and Robert King, eds. *Christian Theology: An Introduction to its Traditions and Tasks*. Third Edition. London: SPCK, 2008.
Irenaeus. *Against Heresies and Fragments (Annotated)*. Kindle Edition. Buffalo: The Christian Literature, 2012.
Kärkkäinen, Veli-Matti. *The Doctrine of God: A Global Introduction*. Grand Rapids: Baker Academic, 2004.
———. *Pneumatology: The Holy Spirit in Ecumenical, International, and Contextual Perspective*. Grand Rapids: Baker Academic, 2002.
Ladd, George E. *The Presence of the Future: The Eschatology of Biblical Realism*. Grand Rapids: Eerdmans, 1974.
Lodahl, Michael. *The Story of God - Wesleyan Theology and Biblical Narrative*. Kansas City: Beacon Hill, 1994.
Luther, Martin. *Sermons of Martin Luther*. Volume 1. Kindle Edition. United States of America: Delmarva, 2014.
Mangina, Joseph L. *Karl Barth: Theologian of Christian Witness*. Aldershot: Ashgate, 2004.

Bibliography

Martyr, Justin, *The Writings of Justin Martyr (Annotated)*. Kindle Edition. Buffalo: The Christian Literature, 2012.
McFague, Sally. *Models of God: Theology for an Ecological, Nuclear Age*. Philadelphia: Fortress, 1987.
McGrath, Alister E. *Christian Theology: An Introduction*. Oxford: Blackwell, 1997.
———. *The Christian Theology Reader*. Oxford: Blackwell, 1995.
———. *Mere Theology: Christian Faith and the Discipleship of the Mind*. London: SPCK, 2010.
———. *Surprised by Meaning: Science, Faith and How We Make Sense of Things*. Louisville, Kentucky: Westminster John Knox, 2011.
McGuckin, John A., ed. *The Westminster Handbook to Origen*. Louisville, Kentucky: Westminster John Knox, 2004.
McIntosh, Mark A. *Divine Teaching: An Introduction to Christian Theology*. Oxford: Blackwell, 2008.
Mechanic, Roni. *A Quest for the Jewish Jesus: Who Do You Say That I Am?* United Kingdom: High Voltage, 2020.
Moltmann, Jürgen. *The Future of Creation: Collected Essays*. Translated by Margaret Kohl. Minneapolis: Fortress, 2007.
Morris, Leon. *I believe in Revelation*. London: Hodder and Stoughton, 1976.
Newbigin, Lesslie. *Faith in a Changing World*. London: Alpha International, 2012.
———. *The Gospel in a Pluralist Society*. London: SPCK, 2004.
Nyssa, Gregory. *Select Works of Gregory of Nyssa*. Kindle Edition. 2016.
Oduyoye, Mercy A. *Daughters of Anowa: African Women and Patriarchy*. New York: Orbis, 2005.
Olson, Roger E. *The Mosaic of Christian Belief: Twenty Centuries of Unity and Diversity*. Downers Grove: InterVarsity, 2002.
———. *The Story of Christian Theology: Twenty Centuries of Tradition and Reform*. Downers Grove: Apollos, 1997.
Origen. *The Complete Works*. Kindle Edition. Toronto, Ontario Canada, 2016.
Otto, Rudolf. *The Idea of the Holy*. London: Oxford University Press, 1958.
Packer, James I. *Knowing Christianity*. Guildford: Eagle, 1995.
———. *Knowing God*. London: Hodder and Stoughton, 1973.
Pannenberg, Wolfhart. *Systematic Theology, Volume 2*. Grand Rapids: Eerdmans, 1994.
Patzia, Arthur G. *The Emergence of the Church: Context, Growth, Leadership and Worship*. Downers Grove: InterVarsity, 2001.
Pink, Arthur W. *The Attributes of God*. Kindle Edition. USA: Dancing Unicorn, 2016.
Plantinga, Richard J. et al. *An Introduction to Christian Theology*. Cambridge: Cambridge University Press, 2010.
Schaff, Philip ed. *The Complete Ante-Nicene & Nicene and Post-Nicene Church Fathers Collection: The Church Fathers*. Kindle Edition. London: Catholic Way, 2014.
Simkins, Ronald. *Creator and Creation*. Peabody, Massachusetts: Hendrickson, 1994.
Stevenson, James, ed. *A New Eusebius*. London: SPCK, 1975.
Tertullian. *Select Works*. Kindle Edition. Toronto, Ontario Canada, 2016.
Torrance, Thomas. *Atonement: The Person and Work of Christ*. Milton Keynes: Paternoster, 2009.
———. *Incarnation: The Person and Life of Christ*. Downers Grove: InterVarsity, 2008.
——— ed. *The Mediation of Christ*. Edinburgh: T&T Clark, 1992.
Walker, Williston. *A History of the Christian Church*. Edinburgh: T&T Clark, 1959.

Bibliography

Walker, Williston et al. *A History of the Christian Church*. Edinburgh: T&T Clark, 1992.
Ward, Keith. *God: A Guide for the Perplexed*. Oxford: Oneworld, 2002.
Wenham, Gordon J. *Genesis* 1-15. Word Biblical Commentary. Nashville: Thomas Nelson, 1987.
Wright, Christopher J. H. *The Mission of God: Unlocking the Bible's grand narrative*. Nottingham: InterVarsity, 2006.
Wright, N. T. *The Challenge of Jesus*. London: SPCK, 2000.
———. *How God became King: Getting to the heart of the gospels*. London: SPCK, 2012.
———. *Who was Jesus?* London: SPCK, 1992.

www.ingramcontent.com/pod-product-compliance
Lightning Source LLC
Chambersburg PA
CBHW072134160426
43197CB00012B/2097